ELLIOTT WAVE PRINCIPLE

FROST and PRECHTER

ELLIOTT WAVE PRINCIPLE
KEY TO STOCK MARKET PROFITS

With a FOREWORD by Charles J. Collins
and an APPENDIX by Walter E. White

Published by NEW CLASSICS LIBRARY

ELLIOTT WAVE PRINCIPLE
KEY TO STOCK MARKET PROFITS

Copyright © 1978, 1981, 1983, 1984 and 1985 by
Robert Rougelot Prechter, Jr. and Alfred John Frost

Printed in the United States of America
by Haddon Craftsmen, Inc., New York City

First Edition: November 1978
Second Edition: January 1981
Third Edition: April 1983
Fourth Edition: July 1984
Fifth Edition: September 1985

For information, address the publishers:
New Classics Library, Inc.
P.O. Box 1618
Gainesville, Georgia 30503

ISBN: 0-932750-07-9
Library of Congress Catalog Card Number: 81-80170

This work is dedicated to the memory of the late A. Hamilton Bolton in appreciation of his great interest in the Elliott Wave Principle as an authentic approach to stock market analysis and the impetus he gave to it during his lifetime.

A Note on the Fifth Edition

The second edition corrected a few typographical errors. The third edition added a Forecast Update (see page 186). The fourth edition corrected the proportions in Figure 69 on page 88. This fifth edition includes a section on the Diagonal Triangle Type 2 on page 48 and added the paragraph and illustrations found on page 100. The rest of the book is intact as it was written in 1978.

ACKNOWLEDGEMENTS

The authors have tried to spell out everything that has been said of Elliott that is worthwhile saying. The book wouldn't be here in its present form, however, without the help of several people whom we will always remember with gratitude. Richard Russell of Dow Theory Letters, who has done much to advance the Elliott theme, first suggested that we write a treatise on the subject. Storey and Boeckh of Bank Credit Analyst fame generously opened their files. Jo-Anne Drew labored hours over the first draft and lent her artistic talents to its production. Mr. and Mrs. Robert R. Prechter, Sr. meticulously edited the final manuscript. Arthur Merrill of Merrill Analysis, Inc. gave us valuable advice and assistance in photography and production. Others too numerous to mention have sustained us in our efforts with advice and encouragement. To all, please accept our thanks.

Background charts for some of the illustrations were provided courtesy of the following sources:

Bank Credit Analyst, Montreal, Canada: figures 55, 78, 85, 100.
M. C. Horsey & Co. Inc., Salisbury, Maryland, 21801: figure 76.
R. W. Mansfield, 26 Journal Square, Jersey City, New Jersey, 07306: figure 12.
Merrill Lynch, Inc.: figures 77, 88, 89, 90, 92, 97.
Securities Research Co., 208 Newbury Street, Boston, Massachusetts, 02116: figures 15, 87.
Trendline (a division of Standard and Poor's Corporation), 345 Hudson Street, New York, New York, 10014: figures 11, 16, 22, 35.

All illustrations not otherwise cited were done by Bob Prechter. The formidable job of lettering and paste-up was patiently performed by Robin Machcinski. The jacket design was crafted by graphics artist Irene Prechter of New Orleans, Louisiana.

The authors have tried to acknowledge all source material used in this book. Any omissions are accidental and will be corrected in future printings if brought to our attention.

CONTENTS

FOREWORD

Some two thousand years ago a man voiced a fe
words whose truth has rung down through the centuries:

One generation passeth away, and another generation cometh, but the earth abideth forever.
The sun also ariseth, and the sun goeth down,
and hasteth to his place where he arose. The
wind goeth toward the south, and turneth about
unto the north; it whirleth about continually,
and the wind returneth again according to his
circuits. All the rivers run into the sea; yet
the sea is not full; unto the flow from whence
the rivers come, thither they return again....
<u>The thing that hath been, it is that which
shall be; and that which is done is that which
shall be done; and there is no new thing under
the sun.</u>

A corollary of this profundity is that human
nature does not change, nor does its pattern. Four men
in our generation have built their reputations in the
economic field on this truth: Arthur Pigou, Charles H.
Dow, Bernard Baruch and Ralph Nelson Elliott.

Hundreds of theories have been advanced
concerning the ups and downs of business, the so-called
business cycle: variation in the money supply, inven-
tory over-balance and under-balance, changes in world
trade due to political edict, consumer attitude, capital
expenditure, even sunspots and juxtapositions of the
planets. Pigou, the English economist, reduced it to
the human equation. The upward and downward swings of
business, Pigou said, are caused by excesses of human
optimism followed by excesses of pessimism. The pendu-
lum swings too far one way and there is glut; it swings
too far the other way and there is scarcity. An excess
in one direction breeds an excess in the other, and so
on and so on, diastole and systole in never-ending
succession.

Charles H. Dow, one of America's most profound
students of stock market movements, noted a certain
repetition in the market's continuing gyrations. Out of
this seeming confusion Dow observed that the market was
not like a balloon plunging aimlessly hither and thither
in the wind but moved through orderly sequence. Dow
enunciated two principles that have stood the test of
time. His first was that the market in its primary

uptrend was characterized by three upward swings. The first swing he attributed to a rebound from the price over-pessimism of the preceding primary downswing; the second upward swing geared into the improving business and earnings picture; the third and last swing was a price overdiscounting of value. Dow's second principle was that at some point in every market swing, whether up or down, there would be a reverse movement canceling three-eighths or more of such swing. While Dow may not knowingly have tied these laws into the influence of the human factor, the market is made by man and continuity or repetition, noted by Dow, necessarily derives from that source.

Baruch, a multi-millionaire through stock market operation and adviser to American presidents, hit the nail on the head in just a few words. "But what actually registers in the stock market's fluctuations," he said, "are not the events themselves, but the human reactions to these events. In short, how millions of individual men and women feel these happenings may affect their future." Baruch added, "Above all else, in other words, the stock market is people. It is people trying to read the future. And it is this intensely human quality which makes the stock market so dramatic an arena, in which men and women pit their conflicting judgments, their hopes and fears, strengths and weaknesses, greeds and ideals."

Now we come to Ralph N. Elliott, who at the time he evolved his theory had probably never heard of Pigou. Elliott had been working down in Mexico but due to a physical malady -- I think he said it was anemia -- had graduated to a rocking chair on a front porch in California. With time on his hands, as he endeavored to throw off his difficulty, Elliott turned to a study of the stock market as reflected by the history and move-ment of the Dow Jones averages. Out of this protracted study Elliott discovered the same repetitious phenomena so eloquently expressed, as quoted in the opening para-graphs of this introduction, by the Preacher of Ecclesi-astes. Elliott, in developing his theory through obser-vation, study and thought, incorporated what Dow had discovered but went well beyond Dow's theory in compre-hensiveness and exactitude. Both men had sensed the involutions of the human equation that dominated market movements but Dow painted with broad strokes of the brush and Elliott in detail, with greater breadth.

I met Elliott through correspondence. I was

publishing a national weekly stock market bulletin to which Elliott wished to join his efforts. Letters back and forth followed but the matter was triggered in the first quarter of 1935. On that occasion the stock market, after receding from a 1933 high to a 1934 low, had started up again but during 1935's first quarter the Dow Railroad Average broke to under its 1934 low point. Investors, economists, and stock market analysts had not recovered from the 1929-32 unpleasantness and this early 1935 breakdown was most disconcerting. Was the nation in for more trouble?

On the last day of the rail list decline I received a telegram from Elliott stating most emphatically that the decline was over, that it was only the first setback in a bull market that had much further to go. Ensuing months proved Elliott so right that I asked him to be my house guest in Michigan over a weekend. Elliott accepted and went over his theory in detail. I could not take him into my organization, however, since he insisted that all decisions be based on his theory. I did help him to locate in Wall Street and in appreciation of his disclosure to me of his work, wrote and put his theory into a booklet entitled The Wave Principle under his name.

Subsequently, I introduced Elliott to Financial World magazine for whom I had contributed and he, through a series of articles, covered the essentials of his theory therein. Later Elliott incorporated The Wave Principle into a larger work entitled Nature's Law. Therein he introduced the magic of Fibonacci and certain esoteric propositions that he believed confirmed his own views.

A. J. Frost and Robert R. Prechter, Jr., the authors of this book, are keen students of Elliott and those who wish to profit by Elliott's discoveries and their application to successful investing will find their work most rewarding.

Charles J. Collins
Grosse Pointe,
Michigan   1978

R. N. ELLIOTT
833-Beacon Avenue
Los Angeles, California
FEderal 2667

Nov. 28, 1934

Mr. C. J. Collins,   PERSONAL
Investment Counsel,   and
Detroit, Mich.   CONFIDENTIAL

Dear Mr. Collins:-,

     For some time I have been trying to formulate this letter, but unable to find expressions that would convey the desired impression and still doubt that I can do so. I am a stranger to you, but feel that I know you through the service letters which I admire very much. On my recommendation some friends have subscribed thereto. I was one of the first subscribers to Mr. Rhea's book and service.

     About six months ago I discovered 3 features in market action, and insofar as I know they are novel. I do not believe that it is egotistical to allege that they are a much needed complement to the Dow theory.

     Naturally I wish to benefit from these discoveries. You have a very extensive following and it has occurred to me that we might reach an arrangement mutually satisfactory. In your letters I have occasionally seen reference to "other sources of information" which prompted me to hope that you might become interested. Moreover from your service letters I judge that you are not familiar with my discoveries.

     Their adoption would in no wise necessitate any reference thereto in service letters. For example when the Dow-Jones Industrials made a top of 107 last April I could have forecasted the 85 bottom and the approximate date it would be reached but your letters could have used the Dow theory as a reason for abandoning long positions. I do not claim that this can always be done. Needless to say the prestige of your service would have materially benefited thereby. Incidently permit me to forecast that the present major bull swing will be followed by a major bear collapse. This is not an opinion but simply the application of a rule.

     These discoveries are much less mechanical than the Dow theory but add great forecasting value which it lacks. One gives reversal signals almost invariably at minor, intermediate and major terminals. Another classifies waves of all movements of which I find six. The other covers the time element which has been 83% correct since the 1932 bottom. When divergence occurs the time element slips out of gear temporarily.

     Unless you contemplate an early visit to the Coast, would you be willing to pay the expense of a trip to Detroit and back ? I know your agent here, Mr. Osbourn, and believe he would give me a "good character", but please note that neither he nor any one else knows anything about my discoveries.

     Yours very truly,

     R. N. Elliott

DEC 2 1934

AUTHORS' NOTE

In co-authoring this book, we have not been unmindful of the little girl who, after reading a book about penguins said, "This book has told me more about penguins than I really care to know." We have tried to explain the basic theory of the Wave Principle in simple terms and avoid, for the most part, areas of dispute.

When presented clearly, the basic tenets of the Wave Principle are easy to learn and apply. Unfortunately the scattered nature of writings on the subject have created problems since there has been no definitive reference text and, in any event, most of the early works are now out of print. In this book we have tried to produce a work which gives a fairly complete treatment of the subject in a manner which we hope will succeed in introducing both experienced analysts and interested laymen to the fascinating field of Elliott.

We trust our readers will be encouraged to do their own research by keeping a chart of hourly fluctuations of the Dow until they can say with enthusiasm, "I see it!" Once the Wave Principle is grasped, the reader will have at his command a new and fascinating approach to market analysis, and even beyond that, a mathematical philosophy which can be applied in other spheres of life. It will not be the answer to all his problems, but it will give him perspective and at the same time enable him to appreciate the strange psychology of human behavior, especially market behavior. Elliott's concepts reflect a principle you can readily prove to yourself and evermore see the stock market in a new light.

A. J. Frost and R. R. Prechter, Jr.

PART I

ELLIOTT THEORY

In The Elliott Wave Principle -- A Critical Appraisal, Hamilton Bolton made this opening statement:

> As we have advanced through some of the most unpredictable economic climate imaginable, covering depression, major war, and postwar reconstruction and boom, I have noted how well Elliott's Wave Principle has fitted into the facts of life as they have developed, and have accordingly gained more confidence that this Principle has a good quotient of basic value.

Ralph Nelson Elliott discovered that the ever-changing stock market tended to reflect a basic harmony found in nature and from this discovery developed a rational system of stock market analysis. He postulated that the price movement of the DJIA (Dow Jones Industrial Average) formed discernable patterns which were repetitive in form, but were not necessarily repetitive in time or amplitude. Elliott claimed predictive value for "The Wave Principle," which now bears the name "The Elliott Wave Principle."

R. N. Elliott's genius consisted for the most part of a wonderfully disciplined mental process, suited to studying charts of the Dow Jones Industrials with such thoroughness and precision that he could construct a network of principles that covered all market action known to him up to the mid 1940's. At that time, with the Dow in the 100's, Elliott predicted a great bull market for the next several decades which would exceed all expectations at a time when most investors felt it impossible that the Dow could even better its 1929 peak. As we shall see, phenomenal stock market forecasts, some of pinpoint accuracy years in advance, have accompanied the history of the development of the Elliott Wave approach.

ONE

THE BROAD CONCEPT

Essentially, the Elliott Wave Principle is a system of empirically derived rules for interpreting action in the major stock market averages. The Wave Principle is a tool of unique value, whose most striking characteristics are its generality and its accuracy. Its generality gives market perspective most of the time and its accuracy in pointing up changes in direction is at times almost unbelievable. Many areas of mass human activity also tend to follow the Wave Principle, but since the stock market as reflected by the DJIA was the basis for Elliott's studies, it is there that the Principle is most popularly applied.

While Elliott had theories regarding the origin and meaning of the patterns he discovered, it should suffice for now that the rules herein have stood the test of time and that market action can be perceived within the context of Elliott's principles. As in much of technical analysis based on chart patterns, it is not necessary to understand immediately the "why," as long as the tools are workable.

In a bull market, the basic objective of Elliott's rules is to follow and to count correctly the development of a five-wave advance in the averages, three up, with two intervening down. This concept should be divorced immediately from the currently popular "all bull markets have three legs" idea, which appears to be a muddled mixture of Dow's three phases and Elliott's five waves. What one might conclude to be a market "leg" in general terms may have any number of different definitions in Elliott terms and may not be a bull "leg" at all. Conversely, a series of "legs" may be interpreted under the Wave Principle to be the completion of only one.

Often one will hear several different interpretations of the Elliott Wave status, especially when cursory, off-the-cuff studies of the averages are made by latter-day experts. However, most uncertainties can be avoided if hourly charts are kept, both on arithmetic and semi-logarithmic chart paper, and if care is taken to avoid breaking any rule whatsoever as laid down by Elliott and later clarified by the late Hamilton Bolton.

Basic Tenets

     In a series of articles published in 1939 by <u>Financial World</u> magazine, Elliott pointed out that the stock market unfolded according to a basic rhythm or pattern of five waves up and three waves down to form a complete cycle of eight waves. The three waves down are referred to as a "correction" of the preceding five waves up. The basic concept of five waves in the direction of the main trend followed by three corrective waves is shown in Figure 1.

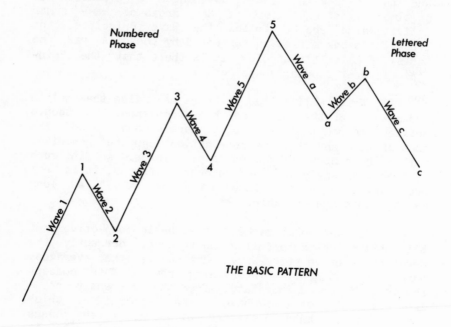

THE BASIC PATTERN

Figure 1

     Waves 1, 3, and 5 are termed <u>impulse</u> waves and waves 2 and 4 <u>corrective</u> waves. Wave 2 corrects wave 1, wave 4 corrects wave 3 and the entire sequence 1, 2, 3, 4, 5 is corrected by the sequence a, b, c. One complete cycle consisting of eight waves, then, is made up of two distinct phases, the numbered phase, sometimes referred to as a "five," and the lettered phase, sometimes referred to as a "three."

     Following this cycle, a second similar cycle of five upward waves begins, followed by another three-waves-down pattern. A third and final advance then develops, consisting of five waves up. At this juncture a major five-wave "up" movement has been completed and a major three-wave "down" movement takes place. These three major waves down "correct" the entire movement of five major waves up. Each of the numbered and lettered "phases" then is actually a wave itself, but of one degree larger than the waves of which it is composed.

This concept is illustrated in Figure 2, showing that two waves of larger degree can be broken into eight waves of the next lower degree, and those eight lower degree waves can be further subdivided in exactly the same manner to produce thirty-four waves of the <u>next</u> lower degree. The Elliott Wave Principle postulates, then, that waves of any degree in any series can always be subdivided and re-subdivided into waves of lesser degree or, conversely, expanded into waves of higher degree. Thus we can use Figure 2 to illustrate two waves, eight waves, or thirty-four waves, depending upon the degree to which we are referring.

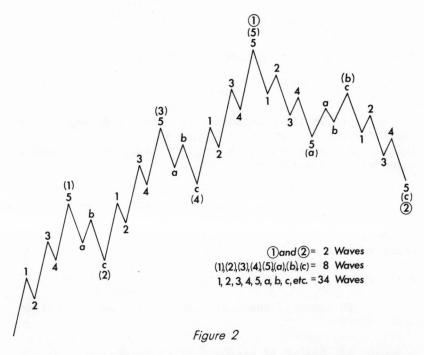

①and② = 2 Waves
(1),(2),(3),(4),(5),(a),(b),(c) = 8 Waves
1, 2, 3, 4, 5, a, b, c, etc. = 34 Waves

Figure 2

The (a)-(b)-(c) corrective pattern illustrated as wave ② in Figure 2 subdivides into a 5-3-5 pattern. Wave (2), if examined under a "microscope," would take the same form as we show for wave ②. Waves (1) and (2) in Figure 2 always take the same form as waves ① and ② , illustrating the phenomenon of constant form within ever-changing degree.

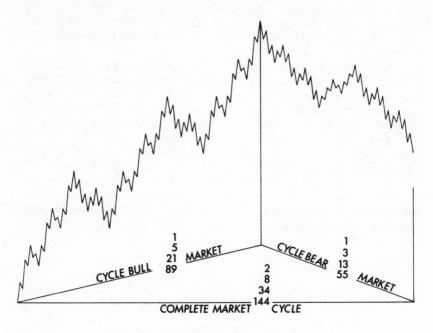

Figure 3

The entire phenomenon of <u>form</u> and <u>degree</u> is carried one step further in Figure 3. Figure 3 illustrates the theory that in a complete stock market cycle, waves will subdivide as follows:

	CYCLE BULL MARKET	CYCLE BEAR MARKET	COMPLETE CYCLE
Cycle Waves	1	1	2
Primary Waves	5	3	8
Intermediate Waves	21	13	34
Minor Waves	89	55	144

In summary, the basic tenets of wave formation are:

1) Action is followed by reaction.

2) Impulse waves, or movements in the direction of the main trend, subdivide into five waves of lower degree and corrective waves, which are movements against that main trend,

whether up or down, generally subdivide into three waves of lower degree.

3) Upon the termination of an eight-wave movement (five up and three down), we have a complete cycle which automatically becomes two subdivisions of the wave of next higher degree.

4) The time frame does not change the pattern, as the market still holds to its basic form. Waves may be stretched or compressed, but the underlying pattern is constant.

Terminology and Labeling

Elliott chose the names listed below in order to classify precisely the nine categories of magnitude discernible to him. They range from the smallest wiggle on an hourly chart to the largest wave he could assume existed from the data then available.

> Grand Supercycle
> Supercycle
> Cycle
> Primary
> Intermediate
> Minor
> Minute
> Minuette
> Sub-Minuette

Although Elliott's terminology shows the mark of genius, the nomenclature of waves is occasionally one of the difficult aspects of the Wave Principle. Waves do not always fit into tight categories and as a result much of Elliott's terminology has never caught the popular imagination. Only the two largest classifications, Grand Supercycle and Supercycle, are used today in the sense Elliott intended them. Categories such as Primary, Intermediate, and Minor have found expression in Elliott literature but are less often used to reflect the exact degree of waves intended by Elliott.

When we refer to the market rise from 1932, we speak of it as a Supercycle with subdivisions as follows:

1932-1937   the first wave of Cycle dimension
1937-1942   the second wave of Cycle dimension

1942-1965(6)   the third wave of Cycle dimension
1965(6)-1974   the fourth wave of Cycle dimension
1974-19??   the fifth wave of Cycle dimension

The subdivisions of each Cycle wave are Primary waves which subdivide into Intermediate waves which in turn subdivide into Minor and sub-minor waves.

When numbering and lettering waves, some scheme such as that shown below is recommended to differentiate the degrees of waves in stock market cycles:

Wave Degree	5's With the Trend					3's Against the Trend		
Grand Supercycle			No practical significance.					
Supercycle	(I)	(II)	(III)	(IV)	(V)	(A)	(B)	(C)
Cycle	I	II	III	IV	V	A	B	C
Primary	①	②	③	④	⑤	ⓐ	ⓑ	ⓒ
Intermediate	(1)	(2)	(3)	(4)	(5)	(a)	(b)	(c)
Minor	1	2	3	4	5	a	b	c
Minute	i	ii	iii	iv	v	-	-	-
Minuette and Sub-Minuette			Use your imagination.					

In Elliott's suggested terminology, the term Cycle is used here only as a name to denote the degree of one size of wave and is not intended to imply a cycle in the currently popular sense. Often, where a wave of either Primary or Cycle dimension has occurred, the term "primary swing" or "primary bull market" is found to have been more commonly used by most analysts since the days of Charles H. Dow, thus posing a problem for new Elliott Wave analysts who might previously have become used to different nomenclature. Since the terminology is not critical to the workings of the system, we suggest the reader use any terms which accomplish his purpose most effectively.

Exactly what constitutes a bull or bear market, furthermore, is a matter of definition. If we think in terms of Elliott's basic concepts, a bull market is a five-wave sequence and a bear market is any corrective sequence. Since a Supercycle "B" wave in a Grand Supercycle correction could last much longer and have a greater amplitude than most Dow Theory "primary" bull markets it would no doubt be referred to by the popular press as a "bull market," despite the fact that under the Wave Principle its correct label would be a bear market rally. In other words, there are widely differing degrees of bull and bear markets under the Wave

Principle. Basically, for Elliott purposes, a bull market is an uptrend comprised of five waves and a bear market is the correction of that uptrend. If nothing else, this concept provides the most precise definition of the terms "bull" and "bear" since Dow Theory.

IMPULSE WAVES --VARIATIONS

Extensions

For the most part, five-wave formations have clear-cut wavelike characteristics with infrequent irregularities except for what are known as extensions. Extensions occur quite often. They are exaggerated or elongated movements which generally appear in one of the three impulse waves (1, 3 or 5). At times the subdivisions of an extended wave are nearly the same amplitude and duration as the other four main waves, giving a total count of nine waves of similar size rather than the normal count of "five" for the sequence. In a nine-wave sequence it is occasionally difficult to say which wave extended, although it is usually irrelevant anyway, since under the Elliott system a count of nine and a count of five have the same technical significance. The diagrams in Figure 4, illustrating extensions, should clarify this point.

The fact that extensions exist can prove a useful guide to the expectable lengths of upcoming waves, since in our experience the majority of waves do contain extensions in one and only one of their three impulse waves. Thus, if the first and third waves are of about equal length, the fifth wave will likely be a protracted surge, especially if volume on the fifth wave is greater than volume on the third wave. Conversely, if wave three has extended, the fifth should be simply constructed and resemble wave one.

Extensions may also occur within extensions. Figure 5 illustrates a span of waves in descending magnitude showing a fifth wave extension of a fifth wave extension. While extended fifths are not uncommon, extensions of extensions occur most often within third waves, as Figure 6 illustrates.

Having cumulatively observed the hourly changes in the DJIA for over twenty years, the authors are convinced that Elliott imprecisely stated some of his findings both with respect to the occurrence of

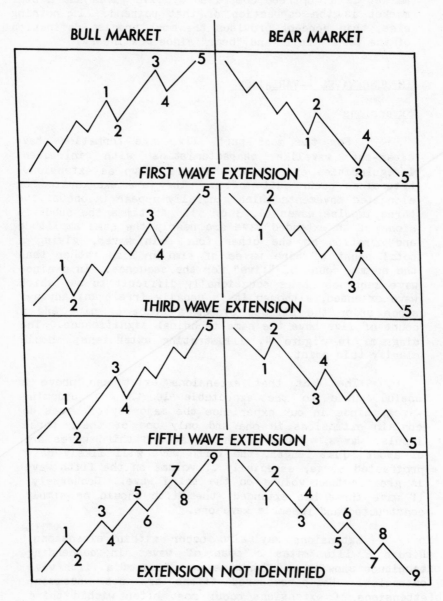

BULL MARKET | BEAR MARKET

FIRST WAVE EXTENSION

THIRD WAVE EXTENSION

FIFTH WAVE EXTENSION

EXTENSION NOT IDENTIFIED

Figure 4

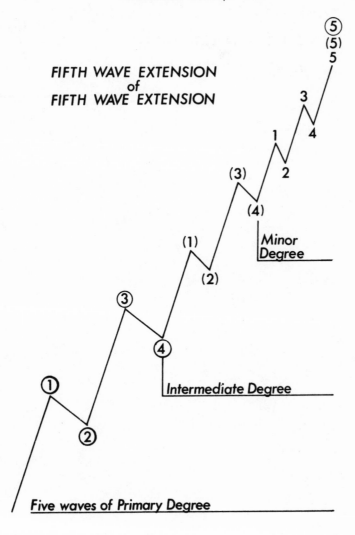

FIFTH WAVE EXTENSION
of
FIFTH WAVE EXTENSION

Minor
Degree

Intermediate Degree

Five waves of Primary Degree

Figure 5

extensions and the market action following an extension. The most important empirically derived rule that
can be distilled from his comments is that when an
extension occurs in a fifth up-wave, the ensuing correction will occur in three waves and retrace to the level
of the beginning of the extension, and be followed by a
second retracement wave which carries into new high
ground for the cycle. That is, fifth wave extensions
are always doubly retraced. The second retracement
marks either the beginning of the next impulse wave of
larger degree (see Figure 7), or, if the previous wave

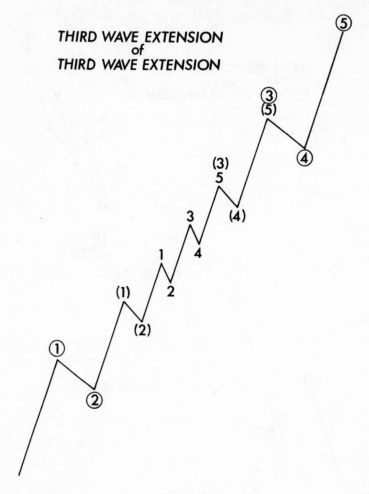

THIRD WAVE EXTENSION
of
THIRD WAVE EXTENSION

Figure 6

of one larger degree was a fifth itself and a major
reversal is due, the first and second retracements will
become waves "A" and "B" of an irregular correction (see
next section), and an irregular top will be formed (see
Figure 8).

The same principle applies in bear markets, but the
illustrations would be inverted.

Our refinements of Elliott's comments, which
appear on page 18 of The Wave Principle (1938), are as
follows:

DOUBLE RETRACEMENT IN A BULL MARKET

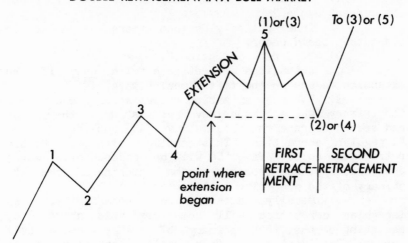

Figure 7

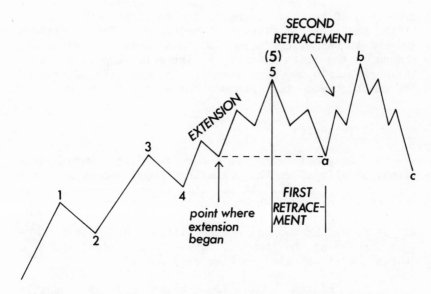

Figure 8

1) "Extensions occur only in new territory of the current cycle."

True, but only because there is no other place they could occur.

2) "Are retraced twice."

Extensions are retraced twice <u>only</u> if the extension occurs in the fifth impulse wave.

3) "When an extension occurs at the end of a 5th primary (where a major reversal is due) the first and second retracements become wave "A" and "B" of an "irregular" correction. This complies with the double retracement rules. Wave "C" will be composed of 5 waves downward, fast and probably to the beginning of the 5th primary of the preceding bull market."

Usually, although not necessarily. An irregular correction will sometimes hold above the beginning of the fifth primary of the preceding bull market. See Chapter 2 in the section on bear market limitations.

4) "An extension is never the end of a movement."

The orthodox end of a "movement" in the direction of the main trend is the terminal point of the fifth wave of a five-wave sequence. What Elliott appears to be saying here is that when an extension occurs in the fifth up-wave, an irregular top will carry the market into new high ground, thereby extending the "movement" beyond the orthodox top of the fifth wave.

Diagonal Triangles

Diagonal triangles occur in fifth wave positions, usually after the preceding move has gone "too far too fast," as Elliott put it. They are a special type of fifth wave which indicate exhaustion of the larger movement. Diagonal triangles are essentially wedges formed by two converging lines, with each subwave, including the impulse waves, subdividing into a "three" as illustrated in Figures 9 and 10.

A rising wedge is bearish and is usually followed by a sharp decline retracing at least back to the level where the diagonal triangle began. A falling wedge by the same token is bullish, usually giving rise to an upward thrust. Diagonal triangles are the only five-wave constructions in the direction of the main trend within which subwave four may, and usually does, fall to a level which is below that of the peak of wave one. Diagonal triangles are fairly rare phenomena and

must not be confused with the more common variety of
corrective triangles which develop in fourth wave positions of impulse waves and wave "B" positions in corrective waves (see next section).

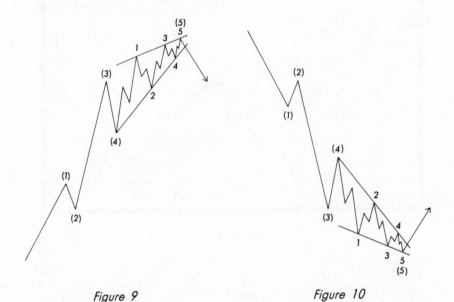

Figure 9   *Figure 10*

        Diagonal triangles have occurred recently in
Minor degree as in early 1978, in Minute degree as in
March 1976, and in Sub-Minuette degree as in June 1976.
Figures 11 and 12 show two of these periods, illustrat-
ing one upward and one downward "real life" formation.

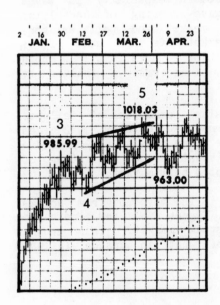

Figure 11

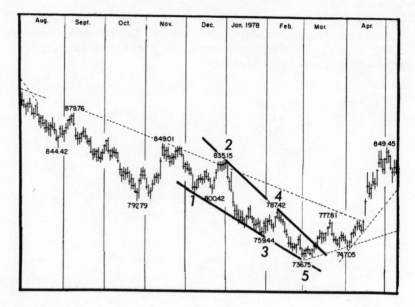

Figure 12

Failures

Elliott used the word "failure" to describe a five-wave pattern of movement in which the fifth impulse wave fails to move above the end of the third. It can usually be verified by noting that the presumed fifth wave contains the necessary five subwaves, as illustrated in Figures 13 and 14.

Failures are not uncommon, especially in waves of small degree. Failures give warning of underlying weakness or strength in the market and tell us more about the reality of stock market life than most of us care to hear. Just when we think we have it all wrapped up in a neat Elliott package, along comes a failure to cut short our expected target.

We have two classical examples of failures since 1932. The first occurred in October 1962 (see Figure 15) at the time of the Cuban crisis and preceded an unusually strong and persistent advance consisting of over five years of uninterrupted bull market.

The second occurred in the move up from November to December 1976 (see Figure 16) and indicated underlying weakness in the stock market. This second failure is a fine example of what an upside failure

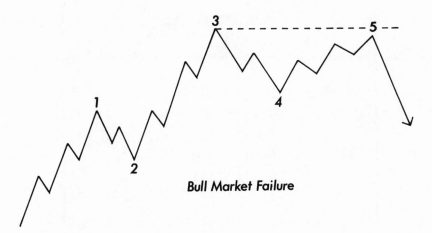

Bull Market Failure

Figure 13

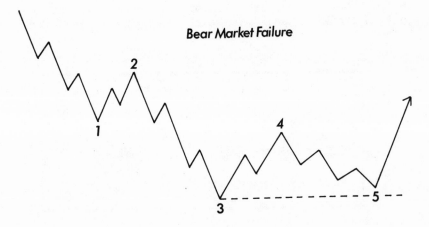

Bear Market Failure

Figure 14

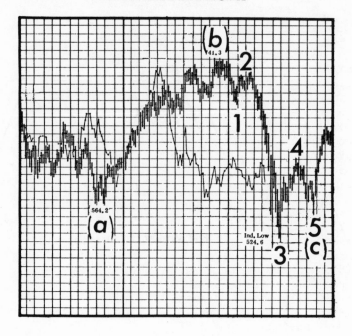

Figure 15

implies. In the ten months following the failure, the
DJIA lacked the strength to mount even one five per cent
rally, almost an unprecedented event. The underperformance of the DJIA compared to the rest of the market was
just as striking and persisted through to the final
bottom.

Figure 16

CORRECTIVE WAVES

Stock market swings of any degree tend to move more easily with the trend of one greater degree than against it. Since corrective waves are generally less clearly identified and subdivided than impulse waves, which flow in the direction of the larger trend, it becomes difficult at times to fit corrective waves into recognizable patterns until they are completed and behind us. As the terminations of corrective waves are less predictable than those for impulse waves, the Elliott analyst must exercise more caution in his analysis when the market is in a meandering corrective mood than when prices are in a positive bull trend. As we shall illustrate, corrective waves are quite a bit more varied than impulse waves. They often increase or decrease in the degree of their complexity as they unfold so that what are technically waves of the same degree can by their sizes appear to be waves of expanding or contracting degree (see Figures 49 and 50 in Chapter 3). This occurrence is analagous to the extension of an impulse wave.

The single most important rule that can be gleaned from a study of the various corrective patterns is that <u>corrections can never be fives</u>. Only impulse waves can be fives. In other words, an initial five-wave movement against the larger trend is never the end of a correction, but only part of it. The following discussion should serve to illustrate this point.

Corrective patterns generally fall into four main categories:

1) Zigzag (5-3-5. Includes the variation "double zigzag").
2) Flat (3-3-5. Includes the variations "irregular" and "running" correction).
3) Triangle (3-3-3-3-3. Four variations: ascending, descending, contracting, expanding).
4) Double three and triple three (combined structures).

Zigzags (5-3-5)

A zigzag in a bull market is a simple three-wave pattern which subdivides into a 5-3-5 affair with the top of wave B noticeably lower than the start of wave A, as illustrated in Figures 17 and 18.

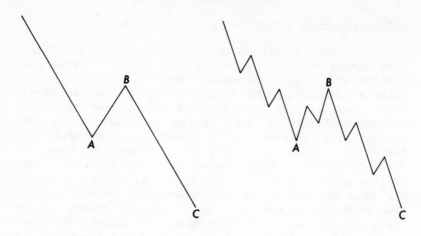

Figure 17   Figure 18

In a bear market, an A-B-C zigzag pattern will be in the opposite direction, as shown in Figures 19 and 20. The position is inverted and for this reason a zigzag in a bear market is often referred to as an inverted zigzag.

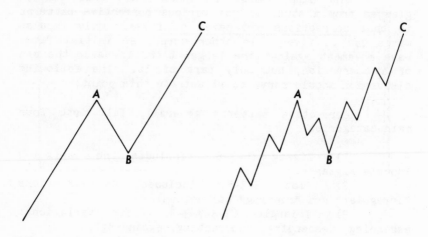

Figure 19   Figure 20

Occasionally in larger formations zigzags can occur twice in succession with an intervening "three," producing what is called a "double zigzag" (see Figure 21). Double zigzags are not common, but occur often enough that the analyst should be aware of their exist-ence. The correction in the Standard and Poor's 500 stock average from January 1977 to March 1978 could be characterized as a double zigzag (see Figure 22).

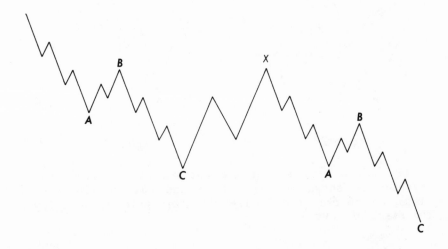

Figure 21

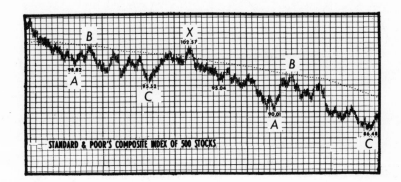

Figure 22

Flats (3-3-5)

A flat type of correction differs from a zigzag in that the subwave sequence is a 3-3-5 affair as shown in Figures 23 and 24. Since the first decline, wave A, lacks sufficient downward force to unfold into a full five waves as it does in a zigzag, the B wave seems to inherit this lack of countertrend pressure and, not surprisingly, often terminates at or above the start of wave A.

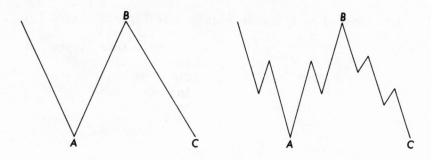

Figure 23

Figure 24

In a bear market the pattern is the same, but inverted as shown in Figures 25 and 26. In inverted flats, of course, the B wave will terminate at or <u>below</u> the start of wave A.

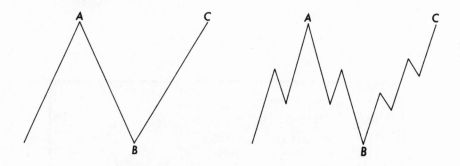

Figure 25

Figure 26

Wave C in any flat generally terminates at or just below the end of wave A rather than significantly below as in zigzags. Thus flat corrections, in their entirety, do less damage to the broader trend. Furthermore, they indicate a strong underlying force in the larger trend and often precede or follow extensions. The longer the flat, the more dynamic is the next impulse wave.

What might be called "double flats" do occur and, in fact, the correction of Cycle dimension which occurred from 1966 to 1974 could be so labeled, as Figure 85 on page 128 illustrates. However, Elliott generally categorized such formations as "double threes," a term which we discuss later in this chapter.

The word "flat" is often used as a catch-all name for any A-B-C correction which subdivides into a 3-3-5. In Elliott literature, however, four types of 3-3-5 corrections have been labeled by differences in their overall shape, which can often be attributed to underlying strength or weakness in the market. In a normal "flat" correction, wave B terminates about at the level of the beginning of wave A, as we have shown in Figures 23-26. However, two types of what are referred to as "irregular" corrections were noted by Elliott.

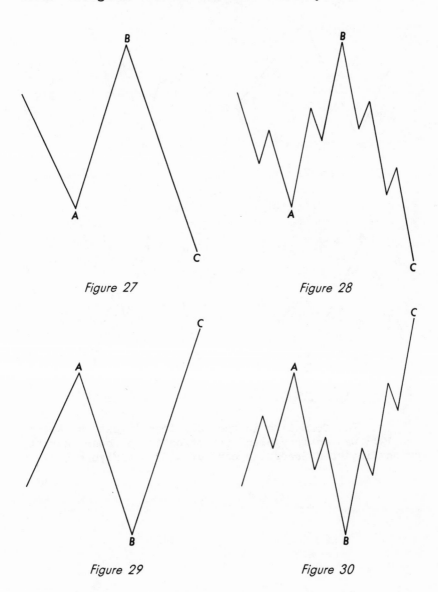

Figure 27

Figure 28

Figure 29

Figure 30

In the first type, wave B of the 3-3-5 pattern terminates <u>beyond</u> the starting point of wave A, and wave C beyond the end of wave A, as shown for bull markets in Figures 27 and 28 and bear markets in Figures 29 and 30.

In the second type, wave B retraces to the beginning of wave A as in a normal flat, but wave C fails to travel its full distance, falling short of the level at which wave A ended, as in Figures 31 through 34.

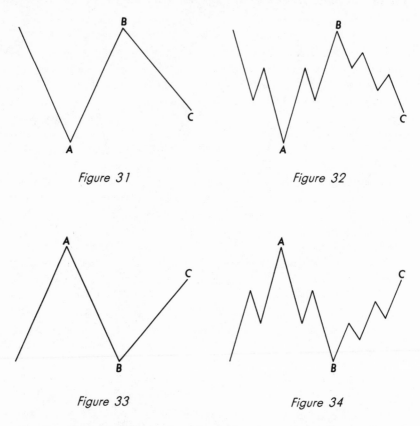

Figure 31   Figure 32

Figure 33   Figure 34

The formation in the DJIA from August to November 1973 was an irregular correction in a bear market, or an "inverted irregular correction" (see Figure 35).

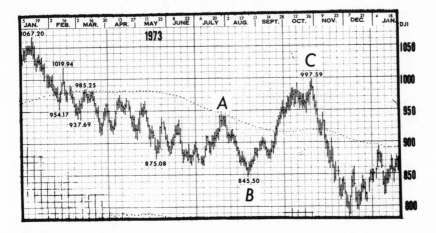

Figure 35

A fourth and final variation on the 3-3-5 structure is the relatively rare "running correction." A running correction in a bull trend is essentially an upwardly skewed A-B-C flat. Apparently the forces in the direction of the larger trend are so powerful that they cause the low of wave C to lie at or above the peak of the previous impulse wave. While running corrections in bull markets indicate great underlying strength, inverted running corrections (those in bear markets) indicate great weakness. Wave (2) in Figure 36 is a running correction.

It is important, when diagnosing a running correction, that the internal subdivisions within the A, B and C waves adhere to Elliott's rules. If the supposed "B" wave, for instance, breaks down into five waves rather than three as in Figure 36, it is more likely the first wave up of the impulse wave of next higher degree. The personality of the wave is important in recognizing running corrections, which tend to occur only in very strong and fast markets, where the market moves so quickly that the corrective patterns do not have time to form properly. At such times the funda-mental or emotional factors seem to be overriding the normal wave development.

Triangles

Triangles as a general rule occur only in posi-tions prior to the final movement in the direction of

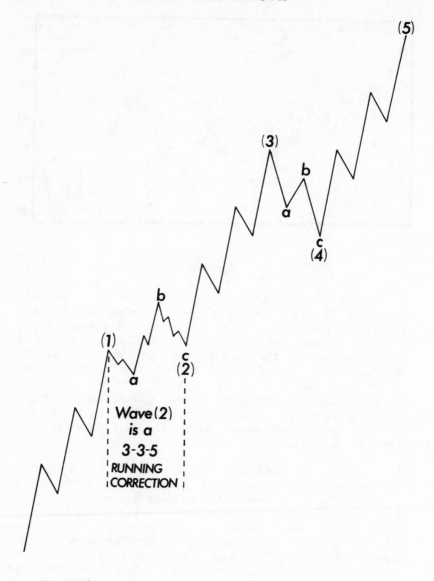

Figure 36

the larger trend. For the most part, they are protracted waves and reflect a balance of forces which creates a
sideways movement that is usually associated with lower
volume and volatility. Triangles are five-wave affairs
which in turn subdivide 3-3-3-3-3. They fall into four
main categories as illustrated in Figure 37.

Corrective Wave (Horizontal) Triangles

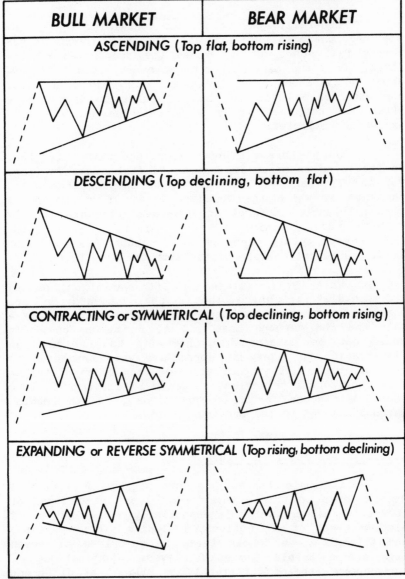

Figure 37

After a triangle is complete, the final impulse wave is generally swift and travels approximately the distance of the widest part of the triangle. Elliott used the word "thurst" in referring to the swift, short impulse wave following a corrective-wave triangle.

Generally, the trendlines containing the triangle are phenomenally accurate in that touch points rarely fall short of or exceed the boundaries of the lines. Only the fifth subwave can be expected to undershoot or overshoot the triangle boundaries and, in fact, our experience tells us that it tends to happen more often than not, especially in contracting triangles and expanding triangles.

On the basis of our experience with triangles, as the later examples in Figures 41 (page 46), 76 (page 96) and 77 (page 97) illustrate, we propose that often the time at which the boundary lines of a previously formed triangle converge at its apex coincides exactly with a turning point in the market. Perhaps the frequency of this occurrence would justify its inclusion among the guidelines associated with the Wave Principle.

While Bolton listed a fifth variation, called "horizontal," in which the triangle boundaries are parallel, Elliott himself never mentioned such a formation and the authors have yet to encounter one. It would not be unacceptable, however, to use such an illustration to represent corrective wave triangles in general, since Elliott called these four types of triangles "horizontal triangles" in order to distinguish them from the diagonal triangle formations of fifth impulse waves discussed in the previous section.

Double Threes and Triple Threes

A single "three" is any zigzag or flat. A double three or triple three is a less common type of corrective pattern which is essentially a combination of simpler types of corrections, including zigzags, flats, and triangles. A double three is comprised of seven legs and a triple three of eleven. Combinations of threes were labeled differently by Elliott at different times, although the illustrative pattern always took the same shape. In Figure 38 the "double three" is composed of seven waves, which can be mentally counted as if saying "a-b-c and a-b-c" or as one through seven.

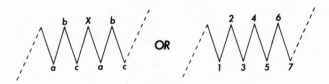

Figure 38

A triple three is illustrated in Figure 39.

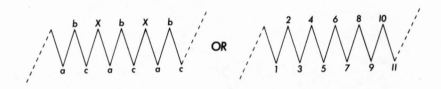

Figure 39

Within a double or triple three formation, the waves in the direction of the previous trend (the even numbers in Figures 38 and 39) always subdivide into threes (or triangles), while those in the direction of the corrective wave can subdivide into threes or fives, depending upon what simpler types of corrective patterns are forming within the structure. In other words, a zigzag followed by a flat, with an intervening three, is one type of double three, as illustrated in Figure 40.

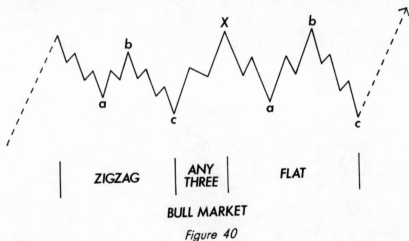

Figure 40

Essentially, the correction from July to October 1975 took this form (see Figure 41).

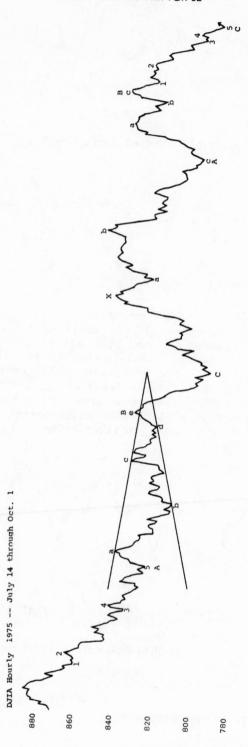

Figure 41

Similarly, as we have mentioned, two juxtaposed flat corrections would also be labeled a "double three," and three juxtaposed flats a "triple three," as Figure 42 illustrates.

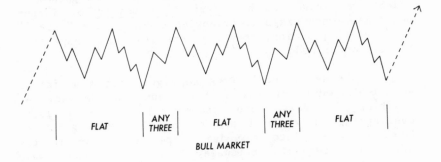

FLAT | ANY THREE | FLAT | ANY THREE | FLAT

BULL MARKET

Figure 42

A double zigzag (see Figure 21 on page 37) could be characterized as a weak, non-horizontal double three, as Elliott seemed to suggest in <u>Nature's Law</u>. Quite often every wave of the entire structure subdivides into a three of some type, as if a horizontal string of zigzags and inverted zigzags were placed side by side, as in Figure 43.

Figure 43

In all of these cases the market is hesitating and acts as if one three weren't enough, as if more time were needed to straighten out whatever "reasons" the market had for pausing in the first place. Sometimes stock prices seem to be waiting for economic fundamentals to begin to catch up with the market's expectations. For the most part, double threes and triple threes are horizontal in character, although Elliott indicated that the entire formations could slant against the larger trend. These formations frequently give rise to strong subsequent action.

Diagonal Triangle Type 2 (A Variation)

By far, most diagonal triangles occur in the "wave 5" position. A small percentage occur in the "wave C" position, but in either case they are phenomena which are found at the <u>termination points</u> of larger patterns. When diagonal triangles occur in the "wave 5" or "wave C" position, they take the 3-3-3-3-3 shape that Elliott described.

It has recently come to light that a variation on the diagonal triangle will be found in the "wave A" position in very rare cases. The characteristic overlapping of waves 1 and 4 <u>and</u> the convergence of boundary lines into a wedge shape remain as in the standard diagonal triangle. However, the wave subdivision is different, tracing out a 5-3-5-3-5 pattern. The structure of this formation (see Figure 44a) does seem to fit the spirit of the Wave Principle in that the five-wave subdivisions in the direction of the larger trend communicate a different message from the "termination" implication of the three-wave subdivisions in a normal diagonal triangle.

This pattern must be noted because it implies only "B" and "C" waves ahead. The analyst could mistake this pattern for a more common development, a series of 1's and 2's (as in Figure 6), which would imply an acceleration of the trend and substantial price movement.

Figure 44b shows a real-life example of the Diagonal Triangle Type 2. We have placed the discussion of this pattern at the end of the chapter because it was not originally discovered by R. N. Elliott.

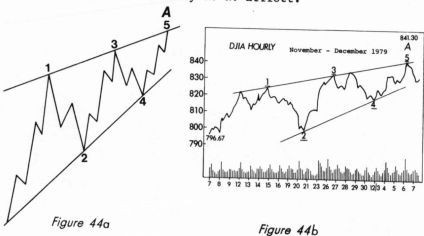

Figure 44a

Figure 44b

Other Patterns

In **Nature's Law**, Elliott referred to a shape called a "half moon." It was not a separate pattern, but merely a descriptive phrase of how a decline within a bear market can begin slowly upon occasion, accelerate, and end in a panic spike. This shape is found more often when prices are plotted on semilog scale.

Also in **Nature's Law**, Elliott twice referred to a structure he called an "A-B base." Elliott invented this pattern during a period in which he was trying to force his Principle into the 13-year triangle concept, which no interpreter today accepts as valid under the rules of the Wave Principle (see THE MAJOR WORKS OF R.N. ELLIOTT, New Classics Library). Indeed, it is clear that such a pattern, if it existed, would have had the effect of flatly invalidating the Wave Principle. The authors have never seen an "A-B base," and have every reason to believe that it cannot exist. It's invention by Elliott merely goes to show that for all his meticulous study and profound discovery, he displayed a typical investor's weakness in (at least once) allowing a prior opinion adversely to affect his objectivity in analyzing the market.

As far as we know, this chapter lists all wave formations which can be constructed in the price movement of the broad stock market averages. Under the Wave Principle, no other formations than those listed here will occur. Indeed, since the hourly readings are a nearly perfectly matched filter for detailing waves of Subminuette degree, the authors can find no examples of waves above the Subminuette degree which cannot be counted satisfactorily by the Elliott method. In fact, waves of even smaller degree than Subminuette are revealed by computer-generated charts of minute-by-minute trading. Even this low number of data bits (transactions) per unit of time is enough to reflect accurately the Wave Principle of human behavior by recording the rapid shifts in psychology occurring in the "pits" and on the trading floor. Now that the elementary rudiments of wave formation have been presented, we can move on to some of the finer points of analysis under the Wave Principle.

TWO

ASSOCIATED RULES AND GUIDELINES

The Rule of Alternation

The rule of alternation touches almost every aspect of the Wave Principle and is a useful rule to keep in mind in analyzing wave formations and assessing future possibilities. The rule tells us to expect alternating patterns in virtually all wave movements. If, for example, corrective wave two is simple, expect the fourth wave to be complex, and vice versa. Figures 45 and 46 show the most characteristic breakdowns of impulse waves, both up and down, as suggested by the rule of alternation. The indications of "simple" corrections usually denote zigzags or simply constructed flats, while those for "complex" corrections can denote triangles, double threes, intricate flats, or any other complex pattern.

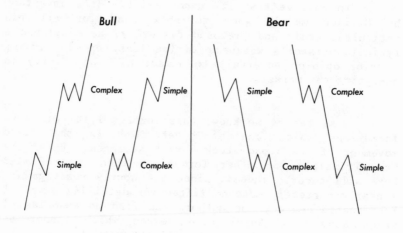

| Bull | Bear |

Figure 45   Figure 46

As another application of the rule, if a large correction begins with a flat a-b-c construction for wave A, expect a zigzag a-b-c formation for wave B, and vice versa (see Figures 47 and 48). With a moment's thought, it is obvious that this rule is sensible, since the first illustration reflects an upward bias in both subwaves while the second reflects a downward bias.

Quite often if a large correction begins with a simple unsubdivided a-b-c for wave A, wave B will stretch out into a complex a-b-c to satisfy the rule of

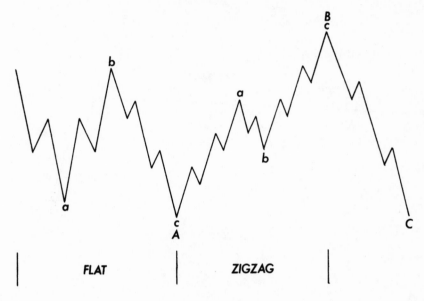

Figure 47

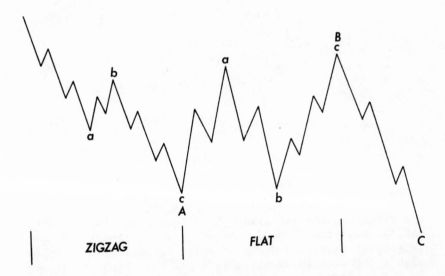

Figure 48

alternation as in Figures 49 and 50. The reverse order of complexity is somewhat less common. An example of its occurrence can be found in wave four in Figure 80, Chapter 3.

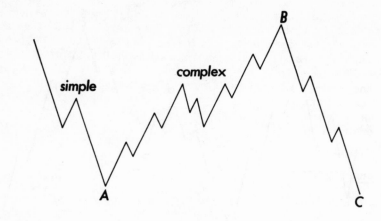

Figure 49

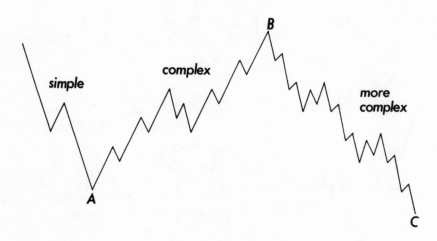

Figure 50

Thus, the rule is very broad in its application and warns the analyst always to expect something different the next time around. At times it applies to slope, length, strength and depth of waves as well as to the clarity of wave movements. An irregular top, generated by a flat correction, is usually next followed by a regular top, and so forth. Hamilton Bolton said:

> The writer is NOT convinced that alternation is INEVITABLE in types of waves in larger formations, but there are frequent enough cases to suggest that one should look for it rather than the contrary.

The rule gives notice of what <u>not</u> to expect, but usually does not say precisely what is going to happen. Its greatest usefulness comes in instructing the analyst not to assume that because the last market cycle behaved in a certain manner, this one is sure to be the same. As "contrarians" never cease to point out, the day that the majority of investors "catches on" to a certain habit of the market is the day it will change to something completely new.

Strength of Trends

Strength of underlying and subsequent trends can often be detected in the structure of wave patterns, particularly corrective patterns, and especially corrective patterns in bear markets, which are usually clearer than those in bull markets. Zigzags, for instance, are indicative of ordinary conditions, while complex corrections indicate a strong underlying or subsequent trend. They usually occur just prior to or immediately following an extension. Figure 51 graphically illustrates the degrees of subsequent strength implied by each of five types of corrections in a bull market. Corrections in bear markets have the same implications as those in bull markets but in the opposite direction.

Correct Counting: Overlapping and Length of Waves

Elliott states in <u>Nature's Law</u> that wave four in a five-wave sequence should not overlap wave one except within diagonal triangles, as discussed in Chapter 1. This is a hard and fast rule which should not be broken unless all other Elliott considerations force the analyst to accept that conclusion. The authors have yet to find one instance in major wave formations when such a forced count was necessary.

Elliott further discovered that the middle wave (3) is often the longest and never the shortest of the three impulse waves in a five-wave sequence, another hard and fast rule which has great practical utility in correct counting. To clarify, let us assume three situations involving a short middle wave as illustrated in Figures 52, 53, and 54.

In Figure 52, wave 4 overlaps the top of wave 1. The count here, subject to a correct breakdown of

STRENGTH IN CORRECTIONS

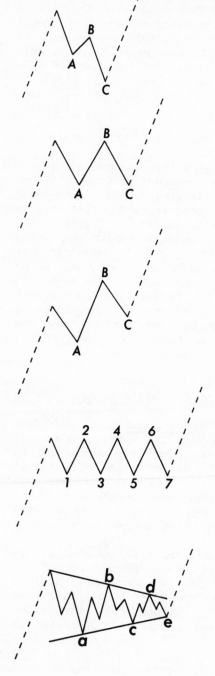

ZIGZAG and DOUBLE ZIGZAG

Ordinary strength.

FLAT and IRREGULAR

Strong.

RUNNING CORRECTION

Unusually strong.

DOUBLE and TRIPLE THREE

Strong.

TRIANGLE

Thrust. Swift but short.

Figure 51

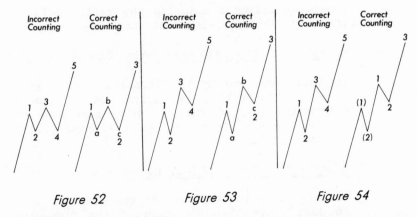

Incorrect Counting	Correct Counting	Incorrect Counting	Correct Counting	Incorrect Counting	Correct Counting

Figure 52   Figure 53   Figure 54

subwaves, would appear to be a normal a-b-c correction. In Figure 53, the middle wave is so short that the entire hesitation, given the correct internal count, could be classified as a running correction. In Figure 54, the "false" wave 4 is well above the top of wave 1, as necessary, but once the wave 5 has traveled further than wave 3, which was already shorter than wave 1, it would be re-labeled as illustrated, implying an extended wave (3) in the making.

Depth of Corrective Waves (Bear Market Limitations)

No market approach other than Elliott gives as satisfactory an answer to the question: How far down can a bear market be expected to go? The answer to this question alone is of sufficient importance to entitle Elliott to a special place in market analysis, as Elliott alone can tell the investor what he can reasonably expect. The rule is that corrections, especially when they themselves are fourth waves, tend to terminate within the span of travel of the previous fourth wave correction of one lesser degree, most commonly near the level of its terminus.

Example #1: The 1929-1932 Bear Market

Our analysis of the period from 1789 to 1932 uses the chart of stock prices adjusted to constant dollars developed by Gertrude Shirk and presented in the January 1977 issue of *Cycles* magazine. Here we find the 1932 Supercycle low bottoming within the area of the previous fourth wave of Cycle degree, an expanding triangle spanning the period between 1890 and 1921 (see Figure 84, page 125).

Example #2: The 1942 Bear Market Low

In this case the Cycle dimension bear market from 1937 to 1942 is a zigzag and terminates within the area of the fourth Primary wave of the bull market from 1932 to 1937 (see Figure 85, page 128).

Example #3: The 1962 Bear Market Low

The big slide in 1962 brought the averages down to just above the 1956 high of the five-wave Primary sequence from 1949 to 1959. Ordinarily the bear plunge would have reached into the fourth Intermediate wave zone. In this case, however, the market had previously built a third wave extension indicating strength in the wave structure, which carried into the construction of the fourth Primary wave (see Figure 85, page 128).

Example #4: The 1974 Bear Market Low

The final decline into 1974, ending the 1966-1974 Cycle dimension wave IV correction of the entire wave III rise from 1942, resulted in bringing the averages down to the area of the previous fourth wave of lesser degree (Primary wave ④). Again, Figure 85 on page 128 shows what happened.

Example #5: London Gold Bear Market, 1974-1976

Here we have an illustration from another market of the tendency for a bear market to terminate in the area of travel of the preceding fourth wave of lesser degree (see Figure 91, page 142).

An empirical analysis of intermediate and minor wave sequences over the last twenty years supports the proposition that the probable limitation of any bear market is in the travel area of the preceding fourth wave of lesser degree, particularly when the bear market in question is itself a fourth wave. However, in a slight modification of the rule, it is often the case that if the first wave in a sequence extends, the

correction following the fifth wave will have as a limit
the bottom of the second wave of lesser degree, as might
logically be expected. The decline into March 1978
bottomed exactly at the low of the second wave in March
1975, which followed an extended first wave off the
December 1974 low.

On occasion, flat corrections or corrections
following extensions will not reach into the fourth wave
area. Zigzags, on occasion, will cut deeply and move
down into the area of the second wave of lesser degree,
although this usually occurs when the zigzags are themselves second waves. "Double bottoms" are sometimes
formed in this manner.

Wave Equality

It is one of the tenets of the Wave Principle
that two of the impulse waves in a five-wave sequence
will tend toward equality in time and magnitude. This
is generally true of the two non-extended waves when one
impulse wave extends and it is especially true if the
third wave is the extension. If perfect equality is
lacking, a .618 multiple is the next likely relationship.

When waves are larger than Intermediate degree,
the price relationships usually must be stated in
percentage terms. Thus, within the entire extended
Cycle wave advance from 1942 to 1966, we find that
Primary wave (1) traveled 120 points, a gain of 129% in
49 months, while Primary wave (5) traveled 438 points, a
gain of 80% (.618 times the 129% gain) in 40 months (see
Figure 85, page 128), far different from the 324% gain
of the third Primary wave, which lasted 126 months.

On the other hand, when the waves are of Intermediate degree or less, the price equality can usually
be stated in arithmetic terms, since the percentage
lengths will also be nearly equivalent. Thus, in the
year-end rally of 1976, we find that wave 1 traveled
35.24 points in 47 trading hours while wave 5 traveled
34.40 points in 47 trading hours. As can be seen, the
rule of equality is often incredibly accurate.

Charting the Waves

A. Hamilton Bolton always kept an hourly chart,
as do the authors. Elliott himself certainly followed

the same practice, since on page 47 of <u>The Wave Princi-</u>
<u>ple</u> he presents an hourly chart of stock prices from
February 23 to March 31, 1938. Every Elliott theorist,
or anyone interested in the Wave Principle, will find it
to his advantage to plot the hourly fluctuations of the
DJIA which are published by The Wall Street Journal and
Barron's. It is a simple task which requires only a few
minutes' work a week. Except when keeping tick-by-tick
charts, the opening market quotations are ignored, as
they represent only the briefest possible trading time.
The so-called "intraday" figures are also ignored, as
they are not a total of component prices at any
particular moment in time, but a sum of the highs (or
lows) of each individual stock in the average,
regardless of the time of day each extreme occurs.

        The foremost aim of wave classification under
the Elliott system is to determine where we are in the
stock market cycle. This exercise is easy as long as
the wave counts are clear, as in fast-moving markets,
particularly impulse waves, when minor movements
generally unfold in an uncomplicated manner. However,
in lethargic or choppy markets, particularly corrections,
wave structures are more likely to be complex and slow
to develop. Complexity and lethargy are two of the most
frustrating occurrences for the analyst, but they are
part of the reality of the market, and must be taken
into account. With a proper reading of "Elliott", there
are many times when sideways trends can be forecasted
(for instance, a fourth wave when wave two was a zigzag).
The authors highly recommend that during such periods
the analyst take some time off from the market to enjoy
the profits made during the rapidly unfolding impulse
waves. You can't "wish" the market into action; it
isn't listening. When the market rests, do the same.

        The correct method for tracking the stock
market is on semi-logarithmic chart paper, since the
market unfolds on a percentage basis. The investor is
concerned with percentage gain or loss, not the number
of points traveled in a market average. For instance,
ten points in the DJIA today means nothing, a one per
cent move. In 1921, ten points meant a ten per cent
move, quite a bit more important. For ease of charting,
however, we suggest using semi-log scale only for long
term plots, when the bias is especially noticeable.
Arithmetic scale is quite acceptable for tracking hourly
waves since a 40 point rally with the DJIA at 900 is not
much different in percentage terms from a 40 point rally
with the DJIA at 1000. Thus channeling techniques work

acceptably well on arithmetic scale with shorter term moves.

Channeling

Elliott used parallel trend channels to assist in determining normal wave targets and to provide clues to possible developement of trends. In The Wave Principle, he asserted that as a wave progresses, "it is necessary that the movement be channeled between two parallel lines." He regarded trend channeling as an important tool in establishing wave completion targets and in the segregation of individual waves.

Elliott contended that the necessity of channeling on semi-log scale indicated the presence of inflation. To date, no student of the Wave Principle has questioned this assumption, which is demonstrably incorrect. Some of the differences apparent to Elliott may have been due to differences in the degree of waves that he was plotting, since the larger the degree, the more necessary a semi-log scale usually becomes. On the other hand, the virtually perfect channels which were formed by the 1921-1929 market on semi-log scale (see Figure 55) and the 1932-1937 market on arithmetic scale (see Figure 56) indicate that waves of the same degree will form the correct Elliott trend channel only when plotted selectively on the appropriate scale. On arithmetic scale, the '20's bull market accelerates beyond the upper boundary, while the '30's bull market on semi-log scale falls far short of the upper boundary.

Regarding Elliott's contention concerning inflation, we note that the period of the '20's actually accompanied mild deflation, as the Consumer Price Index declined an average of .5% per year, while the period from 1933 to 1937 was mildly inflationary, accompanying a rise in the C.P.I. of 2.2% per year. This monetary background convinces us that inflation is not the reason behind the necessity for use of semi-log scale. In fact, aside from the difference in channeling, these two waves of Cycle dimension are suprisingly similar: they both create similar multiples in the stock market (six times and five times respectively), they both contain extended fifth waves, and the peak of the third wave is the same percentage point gain above the bottom in each case.

The essential difference between the two bull

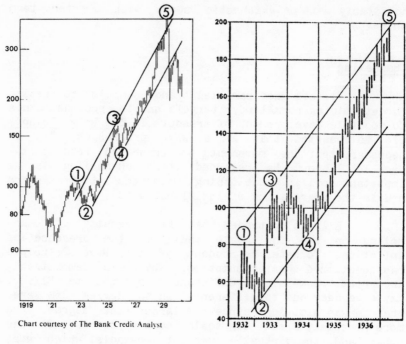

Chart courtesy of The Bank Credit Analyst

Figure 55   Figure 56

markets is the shape and time length of each individual
subwave. At most, we can state that the necessity for
semi-log scale indicates a wave that is in the process
of acceleration. Given a single price objective and a
specific length of time allotted, anyone can draw a
satisfactory hypothetical Elliott Wave channel from the
same point of origin on both arithmetic and semi-log
scale by adjusting the slope of the wave to fit. Thus
the question of arithmetic vs. semi-log scale channeling
is still unresolved as far as developing a definite
tenet on the subject. To stay on top of all developments, the analyst should probably use both.

        The complete channeling technique involves
several steps and revisions. It requires at least three
reference points, which we will label "0," "1" and "2",
before two parallel lines can be drawn.

        The first step uses minimal information and may
be omitted. It requires only the completion of the
first wave. Once the first wave has run its course and
points "0" and "1" are known, a preliminary point "2"
can be established by measuring a point directly below
"1" so that the amplitude between "2" and "1" is 61.8%

of the amplitude of the rise from "0" to "1," as shown in Figure 57.

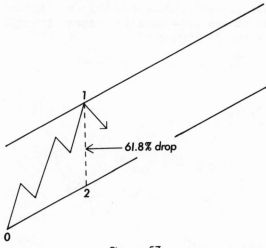

Figure 57

As corrective wave two actually travels towards the lower parallel, it should meet the lower channel boundary in the zone of the previous fourth wave of one lower degree, which not infrequently represents a 50% retracement of the points gained in the rise from "0" to "1." When wave two has bottomed, the channel can be adjusted, if necessary, as in Figure 58.

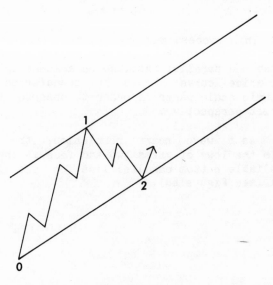

Figure 58

As the wave unfolds, the odds favor the two parallel lines containing the entire up-movement. If a turning point fails to touch or come close to one of the parallel lines, a change of direction of the channel is indicated. To reconstruct the channel, ignore the first exposed point and draw parallel lines through the last three as shown in Figure 59.

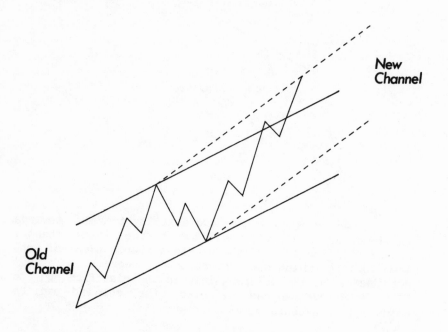

Figure 59

This process may have to be repeated when the fourth wave is completed. If the fourth wave fails to reach the new parallel baseline on arithmetic scale, the entire price curve should be transferred to semi-logarithmic scale paper in order to observe the channel in correct perspective.

As a wave nears completion, the line which connects the lows of waves two and four is the final and most reliable bottom parallel line for the final trend channel (see Figure 60).

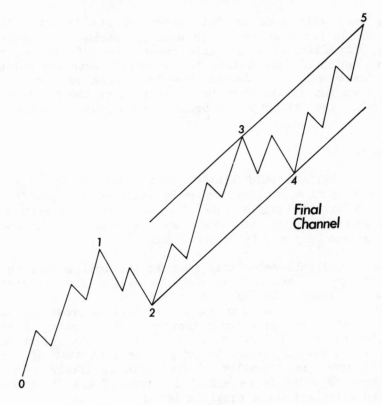

Figure 60

The upper parallel, on the other hand, may have to be adjusted on the basis of one's experience with charting. If waves one and three are not abnormal the upper parallel is most accurate when touching the peak of the third wave, as in Figure 60. If wave three is abnormally strong, almost vertical, then a parallel on top of that third wave may be too high. Past experience has shown that a parallel to the baseline which touches the top of wave one is then more useful, as the illustration of the rise in the price of gold bullion from August 1976 to March 1977 illustrates (see Figure 92, page 143).

When necessary, it may help to draw two upper boundary lines to alert the analyst to be especially attentive to the wave count and volume characteristics at those levels and then take appropriate action as the wave count warrants. In parallel trend channels, if a fifth wave approaches its upper trendline on declining volume, it is an indication that the terminal point of

the wave will meet or fall short of its target. If
volume is heavy as the fifth wave approaches its parallel, it indicates a possible penetration of the upper
line, which Elliott called "throw-over." Near the point
of throw-over, the fourth sub-minor wave of the up-
movement may flatten out immediately below the parallel,
allowing the fifth then to break it on a gust of volume.

Volume

          Elliott said little about volume except that,
in his opinion, it independently followed the patterns
of the Wave Principle. He often used it as a sort of
ancillary tool in verifying wave counts and in the
projection of possible future trends.

          Elliott recognized that in any bull market the
volume has a natural tendency to expand and contract
with the trend. During a corrective phase, a decline in
volume often indicates a decline in selling pressure. A
low point in volume often coincides with a turning point
in the market. Elliott also noted that if the volume on
the fifth wave is equal to or greater than that of the
third wave, an extension of the fifth is likely. This
outcome is often to be expected anyway if the first and
third waves are about equal in length.

          Apart from these few observations, Elliott had
little else to say with respect to volume, although we
have expanded upon its use in various sections of this
book. Generally, however, only to the extent that
volume guides wave counting or expectations can it be
said to have significance.

The "Right Look"

          Although any five-wave sequence can be forced
into a three-wave count by labeling the first three
subdivisions as one wave "A" as shown in Figure 61, it
is incorrect to do so. The Elliott system would break
down if such contortions were allowed. A long wave
three with the end of wave four terminating well above
the top of wave one must be classified as a five-wave
sequence. Since wave A in this hypothetical case is
composed of three waves, wave B would be expected to
drop to about the start of wave A, as in a flat
correction, which it clearly does not. In sum, the
"look" of a wave series is often a guide to its correct

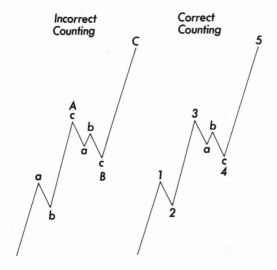

Figure 61

internal count.

    The "right look" of a wave is dictated by all
the considerations we have outlined so far in this
chapter. In our experience, we have found it extremely
dangerous to allow our emotional involvement with the
market to let us accept wave counts which reflect
disproportionate wave relationships merely on the basis
that the Wave Principle is not tied to fixed periodicity. Apart from the irregularities of movement, the
main problem is often with contained waves. When a sub-
minor move is in the price territory of a minor move,
the question often arises as to how the sub-minor move
is to be counted. In such cases, it feels as if the
market is keeping its options open until the fundamentals adjust. Experience with Elliott tells the analyst
that it is better to accept tentatively an unclear wave
as such and wait until the count resolves itself, in
other words, to "sweep it under the rug until the air
clears," as Bolton suggested. If, even in retrospect,
the pattern does not count easily, then the analyst
should consider the pattern as unclassifiable and
proceed from there. Usually, however, subsequent moves
will clarify the status of previous waves by relating to
the wave pattern of the next higher degree. It is our
practice to set targets and try to see in advance where
the next move will likely take the market. The advantage of this practice is that it gives a sort of back-
drop against which to monitor the market's actual path

in order to judge more quickly what went wrong if the market does not do what is expected of it. If you learn the reasons for your past mistakes, the market is less likely to mislead you in the future.

Wave Personality

The personality of each wave in the Elliott sequence is an integral part of the reflection of the mass psychology it embodies. The progression of mass emotions from pessimism to optimism and back again tends to follow a similar path each time around, producing similar circumstances at corresponding points in the wave structure. The personality of each wave type is usually manifest whether the wave is a Grand Supercycle or a Sub-Minuette. These properties not only forewarn the analyst about what to expect in the next sequence but at times can help determine one's present location in the progression of waves, when for other reasons the count is unclear or open to differing interpretations. As waves are in the process of unfolding, there are times when several different wave counts are perfectly admissible under all known Elliott rules. It is at these junctures that a knowledge of wave personality can be invaluable. If the analyst recognizes the character of a single wave, he can often correctly interpret the complexities of the larger pattern.

1) <u>First</u> waves -- As a rough estimate, about half of first waves are part of the "basing" process and thus tend to be heavily corrected by wave two. In contrast to the bear market rallies within the previous decline, however, this first wave rise is less emotional and technically more constructive. Plenty of selling, including short selling, is in evidence as the majority has finally become convinced that the overall trend is down. The other fifty per cent of first waves rise from either extremely large bases formed by the previous correction, as in 1949, from downside failures, as in 1962, or from extreme compression as in both 1962 and 1974. From these beginnings, first waves are impressively dynamic.

2) <u>Second</u> waves -- Second waves often retrace so much of wave one that most of the profits gained up to that time are eroded away by the time it ends. This is especially true of call option purchases, as premiums sink drastically in the stepped-up selling during second

waves. Investors have finally gotten "one more rally to sell on" and they take advantage of it. Second waves often produce downside non-confirmations and Dow Theory "buy spots," when low volume and volatility indicate a dry-up of selling pressure.

3) <u>Third</u> waves -- Third waves are wonders to behold. They are strong and broad, and the trend at this point is unmistakable. Increasingly favorable fundamentals enter the picture as confidence returns. Third waves usually generate the greatest volume and price movement and are most often the extended wave in a series. It follows, of course, that the third wave of a third wave, and so on, will be the most volatile point of strength in any wave sequence. Such points invariably produce breakouts, breakdowns, runaway gaps, volume expansions, exceptional breadth, thrust, major Dow Theory trend confirmations and large hourly, daily, weekly, monthly or yearly moves in the market, depending on the degree of the wave. Virtually all stocks participate in third waves. Besides the personality of "B" waves, that of third waves produces the most valuable clues to the wave count as it unfolds.

4) <u>Fourth</u> waves -- Fourth waves are predictable to the extent that, by rule of alternation, they should differ in complexity from the previous second wave of the same degree. More often than not they are complex waves, building the base for the final fifth wave move. Lagging stocks in an up-cycle build their tops and begin declining during this wave, since only the strength of a third wave was able to generate any motion in them in the first place. This initial deterioration in the market sets the stage for non-confirmations and subtle signs of weakness during the fifth wave.

5) <u>Fifth</u> waves -- Fifth waves are usually less dynamic than popular conception holds. Most Elliott dabblers are reminded of 1928-1929 and assume that fifth waves are "blowoff" types. However, the average fifth wave is almost always less impressive than the third, unless it constitutes an extension. During fifth advancing waves, optimism runs extremely high and secondary stocks participate widely and in a healthy manner. As an example, the year-end rally in 1976, a fifth wave in the DJIA, actually was <u>led</u> by secondary stocks. The wave itself was unexciting in the Dow, but it was nevertheless an impulse wave, as opposed to the preceding corrective wave advances in April, July and September,

which, by contrast, had little influence on the secondary indexes or the cumulative advance-decline line. As a monument to the optimism which that rally produced, the advisory services polled two weeks after its conclusion turned in the lowest percentage of "bears," 4.5%, in the history of the recorded figures.

6) "A" waves -- During A waves of bear markets, the investment world is generally convinced that this reaction is just a minor pullback pursuant to the next leg of advance. The odd-lot public surges to the buy side, despite the first really technically damaging cracks in individual stock patterns. The A wave sets the tone for the B wave to follow. Flat A's precede upwardly zigzagging B's and zigzagging A's precede flat B's.

7) "B" waves -- Upward B waves are phonies. They are sucker plays, bull traps, speculators' paradise, orgies of odd-lotter mentality. They are often emotional, rarely technically strong, and virtually always doomed to complete retracement by wave C. If the analyst can easily say to himself, "There is something wrong with this market," chances are it's a B wave. Several examples will suffice to illustrate the point.

     -- The upward correction of 1930 was a B wave within the 1929-1932 A-B-C zigzag decline. Robert Rhea describes the emotional climate well in his opus The Story of the Averages (1934):

> ...many observers took it to be a bull market signal. I can remember having shorted stocks early in December, 1929 after having completed a satisfactory short position in October. When the slow but steady advance of January and February carried above [the previous high] , I became panicky and covered at considerable loss. ...I forgot that the rally might normally be expected to retrace possibly 66 per cent or more of the 1929 downswing. Nearly everyone was proclaiming a new bull market. Services were extremely bullish, and the upside volume was running higher than at the peak in 1929.

     -- The 1961-1962 rise was a B wave in a large A-B-C irregular correction. At the top in early 1962, stocks were selling at unheard of price/earnings multiples that had not been seen up to that time and have not been seen since. Cumulative breadth had peaked along with the top of the third wave in 1959.

-- The rise into the 1968 peak was a corrective wave advance in the DJIA. Emotionalism had gripped the public and "cheapies" were skyrocketing in the speculative fever, unlike the orderly and usually fundamentally justifiable participation of the secondaries within fifth waves. The Dow Industrials struggled unconvincingly higher throughout the wave and finally refused to confirm the phenomenal new highs in the secondary indexes.

-- The rise off the 1970 low into January 1973 was another corrective wave advance within the large wave IV of Cycle degree. The "one-decision" euphoria which held the average institutional fund manager is well documented. The area of participation · again was narrow, this time the "nifty fifty" growth and glamour issues rather than the secondaries. Breadth, as well as the Transportation Average, topped early, in 1972, and refused to confirm the phenomenal multiples bestowed upon the favorite fifty. Washington was inflating at full steam to sustain the illusory prosperity during the entire advance in preparation for the election. Again, "phony" was an apt description.

--In 1977, the Dow Jones Transportation Average climbed to new highs in a B wave, miserably unconfirmed by the Industrials. Airlines and truckers were sluggish. Only the coal-carrying rails were participating as part of the energy play. Thus breadth within the index was conspicuously lacking, confirming again that good breadth is generally a property of impulse waves, not corrections.

-- For a discussion of the B wave in the gold market, see Chapter 6, pages 141-142.

As a general observation, "B" waves of Intermediate degree and lower usually show a diminution of volume, while "B" waves of Primary degree and greater often display volume noticeably heavier than that which accompanied the preceding bull market, usually as an indication of wide public participation.

8) "C" waves -- Declining C waves are usually devastating in their destruction. They are third waves, and have most of the properties of third waves. It is during this decline that there is virtually no place to hide except cash. The illusions held throughout waves A

and B tend to evaporate and fear takes over. C waves
are persistent and broad. 1930-1932 was a C wave. 1962
was a C wave. 1969-1970 and 1973-1974 can be classified
as C waves. Advancing C waves within upward corrections
in larger bear markets are just as dynamic and might
often be mistaken for the start of a new upswing, especially since they unfold in five waves. The October 1973
preoil embargo rally (see Chapter 1, Figure 35), for
instance, was a C wave in an inverse irregular correction.

    These personality categories are for the most
part suggestive, not inevitable and thus not stated as
rules, but as guidelines. There are always exceptions
to the guidelines but without those, market analysis
would be a science, not an art. With a thorough knowledge of wave characteristics, however, the analyst is
that much more confident of his wave count. In effect,
one can use the market action to confirm the wave count
as well as use the wave count to predict market action.

Learning the Basics

    With the tools in this chapter, most students
can grasp Elliott very quickly. Without them, most
people give up before they give it a real try. The best
learning procedure is to keep an hourly chart and try to
fit all the boggles into Elliott wave patterns, while
keeping an open mind for all the possibilities. Slowly
the scales should drop from your eyes and you continually will be amazed at what you see.

    It is important to remember that while invest-
ing tactics always must go with the most valid wave
count, knowledge of the alternatives can be extremely
helpful in interpreting unexpected events, putting them
immediately into perspective and adapting to the changing market framework. While the rigidities of Elliott
rules are of great value in choosing entry and exit
points, the flexibilities in the admissible patterns
eliminate cries that whatever the market is doing now is
"impossible."

    "When you have eliminated the impossible, what-
ever remains, however improbable, must be the truth."
Thus eloquently spoke Sherlock Holmes to his constant
companion, Dr. Watson, in Arthur Conan Doyle's The Sign

<u>of the Four</u>. This one sentence of advice is a capsule
summary of what one needs to know to be successful with
Elliott. The best approach is deductive reasoning. By
knowing what Elliott rules will not allow, one can
deduce that whatever remains must be the most likely
course of the market. Applying all the rules of extensions, alternation, overlapping, channeling, volume and
the rest, the analyst has a much more formidable arsenal
than one might imagine at first glance. Unfortunately
for many, the approach requires thought and work, and
rarely provides a mechanical signal. However, this kind
of thinking, basically an elimination process, squeezes
the best out of what Elliott has to offer and besides,
it's fun! We sincerely urge you to give it a try.

Christopher Morley once said, "Dancing is a
wonderful training for girls. It is the first way they
learn to guess what a man is going to do before he does
it." In the same way Elliott trains the analyst to
discern what the market is likely to do before it does
it.

After you have acquired an Elliott "touch," it
will be forever with you, just as a child who learns to
ride a bicycle never forgets. At that point, catching a
turn becomes a fairly common experience and not really
too difficult. Most importantly, in giving the investor
the feeling of confidence as to where he is in the
progress of the market, a knowledge of Elliott can
psychologically prepare him for the inevitable fluctu-
ating nature of price movement and free him from the
pitfall of linear thinking.

Despite the fact that many analysts do not
treat it as such, Elliott is by all means an objective
study, or as Collins put it, "a disciplined form of
technical analysis." Bolton used to say that one of the
hardest things he had to learn was to believe what he
saw. If the analyst does not believe what he sees he is
likely to read into his analysis what he thinks should
be there for some other reason. At this point the count
becomes subjective. Subjective analysis is dangerous
and destroys the objectivity of any market approach. If
the waves are open to interpretations at times as all
indicators are, one should reserve final judgment since
subsequent waves virtually always clarify the picture.
On the other hand, sometimes the ability to assess the
<u>degree</u> of the turn and thus predict the extent of the
ensuing wave, can be a stumbling block. Although
prediction of target levels well in advance can be done

surprisingly often, such prediction can be irrelevant to
making money trading the stock market.   All one really
needs to know at the time is whether to be long or short.

Of the many approaches to stock market analysis, the Elliott Wave Principle, in our view, offers the
best tool for identifying market turns as they are
approached. If you keep an hourly chart, the fifth of
the fifth of the fifth in a primary trend brings you
within hours of a change of direction in the market.   It
is a thrilling experience to pinpoint a turn, but never
get hooked on the Principle so deeply that you refuse to
recognize other technical tools. Elliott is not the
perfect formulation, since the stock market is part of
life and no formula can enclose it or give complete
expression to it. The Wave Principle, however, is a
fascinating approach to market analysis and, viewed in
its proper light, delivers everything it promises.

THREE

HISTORICAL AND MATHEMATICAL BACKGROUND OF THE WAVE PRINCIPLE

The Fibonacci (pronounced FI-BO-NA'-CHEE) sequence of numbers was discovered by Leonardo Fibonacci da Pisa, a thirteenth century mathematician. We will outline the historical background of this amazing man and then discuss more fully the sequence of numbers (technically it is a sequence and not a series) which bears his name. When Elliott wrote <u>Nature's Law</u>, he referred specifically to the Fibonacci sequence as the mathematical basis for the Wave Principle. It is suffi- cient to state at this point that the stock market has a propensity to demonstrate a form which can be aligned with the form present in the Fibonacci sequence. For a further discussion of the mathematics behind the Wave Principle see our Appendix, "Mathematical Basis of Wave Theory" by Walter E. White.

Leonardo Fibonacci da Pisa

The Dark Ages was a period of almost total eclipse in Europe when learning became virtually extinct. The age lasted from the fall of Rome in 476 A.D. to the beginning of the Middle Ages around 1000 A.D. During this period, mathematics and philosophy waned in Europe but flowered in India and Arabia, since the Dark Ages, as such, did not exist in the East. As Europe gradually began to emerge from its stagnant state, the Mediterranean Sea developed into a river of history which directed the flow of commerce, mathematics and new ideas from India and Arabia.

During the early Middle Ages, Pisa became a strongly-walled city-state and a flourishing commercial and trading center whose waterfront reflected the Commercial Revolution of that day. Leather, furs, cotton, wool, iron, copper, tin and spices were traded within the walls of Pisa, with gold serving as an impor- tant currency. The port was filled with ships ranging up to four hundred tons and eighty feet in length. The Pisan economy supported a leather and shipbuilding industry and an iron works. Pisan politics were well constructed, even according to today's standards. The Chief Magistrate of the Republic, for instance, was not paid for his services until after his term of office had expired, at which time his administration could be investigated to determine if he had earned his salary. In fact, our man Fibonacci was one of the examiners.

Born between 1170 and 1180, Leonardo Fibonacci, the son of a prominent merchant and city official, probably lived in one of Pisa's many towers. A tower served as a workshop, fortress and family residence and was so constructed that arrows could be shot from the narrow windows and boiling tar poured on strangers who approached with aggressive intent. During Fibonacci's lifetime, the bell tower known as the Leaning Tower of Pisa was under construction. It was the last of the three great edifices to be built in Pisa, as the cathedral and the baptistery had been completed some years earlier.

As a school boy, Leonardo became familiar with customs houses and commercial practices of the day, including the operation of the abacus which was widely used in Europe as a calculator for business purposes. Although his native tongue was Italian, he learned several other languages, including French, Greek and even Latin, in which he was fluent.

Soon after Leonardo's father was appointed a customs official at Bogia in North Africa, he instructed Leonardo to join him in order to complete his education, during which time Leonardo made many business trips around the Mediterranean. Then, after one of his trips to Egypt, he published his famous <u>Liber Abaci</u> (Book of Calculations) which introduced to Europe one of the greatest mathematical discoveries of all time, namely the decimal system, including the positioning of zero as the first digit in the notation of the number scale. The system which included the familiar symbols 0, 1, 2, 3, 4, 5, 6, 7, 8, and 9 became known as the Hindu-Arabic system which is now universally used.

Under a true digital or place-value system, the actual value represented by any symbol placed in a row along with other symbols depends not only on its basic numerical value but also on its position in the row, i.e., 58 has a different value from 85. Though thousands of years earlier the Babylonians and Mayans of Central America separately had developed digital or place-value systems of numeration, their methods were awkward in other respects. For this reason the Babylonian system, which had been the first to use zero and the place-values of symbols, was never carried forward into the mathematical systems of Greece, or even Rome, whose numeration was comprised of the seven symbols I, V, X, L, C, D, and M, with non-digital place-values assigned to those symbols. Addition, subtraction, multiplication and division in a system using these non-digital symbols is not an easy task, especially where large numbers are involved. Paradoxically, to overcome this problem, the Romans used the very ancient digital device known as the abacus. Because this instrument is digitally based and contains the zero principle, it functioned as a necessary supplement to the Roman computational system. Throughout the ages, bookkeepers and merchants depended on it to assist them in the mechanics of their tasks. Fibonacci, after verbally expressing the basic principle of the abacus in <u>Liber Abaci</u>, started to use his new system during his travels and, through his writings, eventually transmitted the new system to Europe with its easy method of calculation. Gradually the old usage of Roman numerals was replaced with the Arabic numeral system. The introduction of the new system to Europe was the first important achievement in the field of mathematics after the fall of Rome over seven hundred years before. Fibonacci not only kept mathematics alive during the Middle Ages, but laid the foundation for great developments in the field of higher mathematics and the related fields of physics, astronomy and engineering.

Although the world later almost lost sight of Fibonacci, he was unquestionably a man of his time. His fame was such that Frederick II, a scientist and scholar in his own right, sought him out by arranging a visit to Pisa. Frederick II was Emperor of the Holy Roman Empire, the King of Sicily and Jerusalem, scion of two of the noblest families in Europe and Sicily, and the most powerful prince of his day. His ideas were those of an absolute monarch and he surrounded himself with all the pomp of a Roman emperor.

The meeting between Fibonacci and Frederick II took place in 1225 A.D. and was an event of great importance to the town of Pisa. The Emperor rode at the head of a long procession of trumpeters, courtiers, knights, officials and a menagerie of animals. Some of the problems the Emperor placed before the famous mathematician are detailed in <u>Liber Abaci</u>. Fibonacci apparently solved the problems posed by the Emperor and forevermore was welcome at the King's Court. When Fibonacci revised <u>Liber Abaci</u> in 1228 A.D., he dedicated the revised edition to Frederick II.

It is almost an understatement to say that Leonardo Fibonacci was the greatest mathematician of the Middle Ages. In all, he wrote three major mathematical works: the Liber Abaci, published in 1202 and revised in 1228, Practica Geometriae, published in 1220, and Liber Quadratorum. The admiring citizens of Pisa documented in 1240 A.D. that he was "a discreet and learned man," and very recently Joseph Gies, a senior editor of the Encyclopedia Britannica, stated that future scholars will in time "give Leonard of Pisa his due as one of the world's great intellectual pioneers." His works, after all these years, are only now being translated from Latin into English. For those interested, the book entitled Leonard of Pisa and the New Mathematics of the Middle Ages, by Joseph and Frances Gies, is an excellent treatise on the age of Fibonacci and his works.

Although he was the greatest mathematician of medieval times, Fibonacci's only monuments are a small statue across the Arno River from the Leaning Tower and two streets which bear his name, one in Pisa and the other in Florence. It seems strange that so few visitors to the 179-foot marble Tower of Pisa, which leans seventeen feet out of the perpendicular, have ever heard of Fibonacci or seen his statue. Fibonacci was a contemporary of Bonanna, the architect of the Tower, who started building in 1174 A.D. The two men made great contributions to the world but the one whose influence far exceeds the other's is almost unknown.

The Fibonacci Sequence

In Liber Abaci, a problem is posed which gives rise to the sequence of numbers 1, 1, 2, 3, 5, 8, 13, 21, 34, 55, 89, 144, and so on to infinity, known today as the Fibonacci sequence. The problem is:

> How many pairs of rabbits placed in an enclosed area can be produced in a single year from one pair of rabbits if each pair gives birth to a new pair each month starting with the second month?

In arriving at the solution, we find that each pair, including the first pair, needs a month's time to mature, but once in production, begets a new pair each month. The number of pairs is the same at the beginnings of each of the first two months, so the sequence is 1, 1. This first pair finally doubles its number

THE RABBIT FAMILY TREE

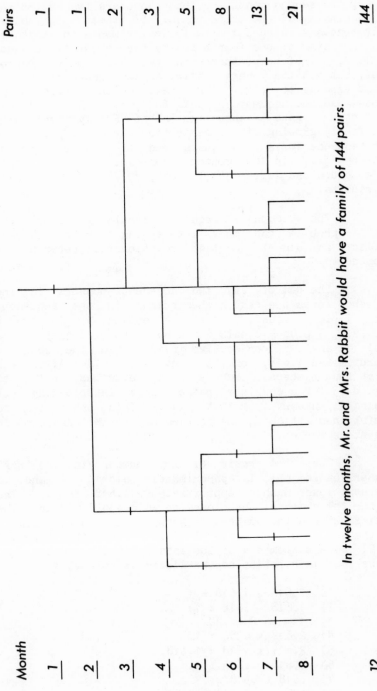

In twelve months, Mr. and Mrs. Rabbit would have a family of 144 pairs.

Figure 62

during the second month, so that there are two pairs at
the beginning of the third month. Of these, the older
pair begets a third pair the following month so that at
the beginning of the fourth month, the sequence expands
1, 1, 2, 3. Of these three, the two older pairs repro-
duce, but not the youngest pair, so the number of rabbit
pairs expands to five. The next month, three pairs
produce so the sequence expands to 1, 1, 2, 3, 5, 8 and
so forth. Figure 62 shows the Rabbit Family Tree with
the family growing with logarithmic rapidity. Continue
the sequence for a few years and the numbers become
astronomical. In 100 months, for instance, we would
have to contend with 354,224,848,179,261,915,075 pairs
of rabbits.

The Fibonacci sequence resulting from the
rabbit problem has many interesting properties and
reflects an almost constant relationship between its
components.

The sum of any two adjacent numbers in the
sequence forms the next higher number in the sequence,
viz., 1 plus 1 equals 2, 1 plus 2 equals 3, 2 plus 3
equals 5, 3 plus 5 equals 8 and so on to infinity. The
ratio of any two consecutive numbers in the sequence
approximates 1.618, or its inverse, .618, after the
first four numbers. For specific examples, refer to
Figure 63 for a complete ratio table interlocking all
Fibonacci numbers from 1 to 144. This table can be
useful when attacking the problem of ratio analysis in
the stock market.

Thus the ratio of any number to the next
higher, called phi, is approximately .618 to 1 and to
the next lower number approximately 1.618 to 1. The
higher the numbers, the closer to .618 and 1.618 are the
ratios between the numbers. Between alternate numbers
in the sequence, the ratio is 2.618, or its inverse,
.382. Some statements of the interrelated properties of
these four main ratios can be listed as follows:

      1)   2.618 - 1.618 = 1.
      2)   1.618 - .618 = 1.
      3)   1 - .618 = .382.
      4)   2.618 x .382 = 1.
      5)   2.618 x .618 = 1.618.
      6)   1.618 x .618 = 1.
      7)   .618 x .618 = .382.
      8)   1.618 x 1.618 = 2.618.

Fibonacci Ratio Table

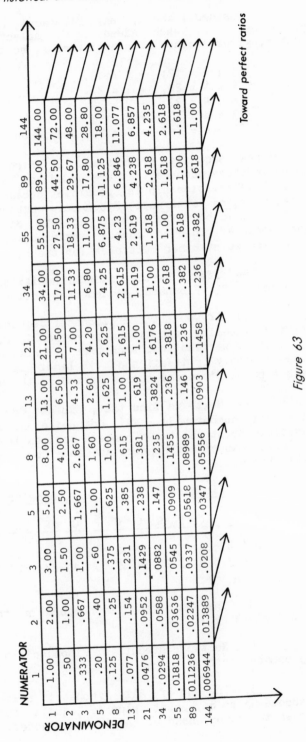

Figure 63

Besides 1 and 2, any Fibonacci number multiplied by four, when added to a selected Fibonacci number, gives another Fibonacci number, so that:

```
 3 x 4 = 12;   + 1 = 13.
 5 x 4 = 20;   + 1 = 21.
 8 x 4 = 32;   + 2 = 34.
13 x 4 = 52;   + 3 = 55.
21 x 4 = 84;   + 5 = 89, and so on.
```

As the new sequence progresses, a third sequence is begun in those numbers that are added to the 4x multiple. This relationship is possible because the ratio between <u>second</u> alternate Fibonacci numbers is 4.236, where .236 is both its inverse <u>and</u> its difference from the number 4. This continuous series-building property is reflected at other multiples for the same reasons.

We offer a partial list of additional phenomena relating to the Fibonacci sequence as follows:

1) If we list the Fibonacci sequence and count forward, labeling each Fibonacci number 1, 2, 3, 4, 5, 6, 7, etc., we find that each time a prime number (one divisible only by itself and 1) label is reached, we have a prime Fibonacci number listed in the sequence.

2) Next, we find that, except for the fourth Fibonacci number (3), all composite numbers (those divisible by at least two numbers besides themselves and 1) label composite Fibonacci sequence numbers, as in the table below.

Fibonacci: Prime vs. Composite

<u>P</u>	<u>P</u>	<u>P</u>	<u>X</u>	<u>P</u>	<u>C</u>	<u>P</u>	<u>C</u>	<u>C</u>	<u>C</u>	<u>P</u>	<u>C</u>	<u>P</u>	<u>C</u>	<u>C</u>	<u>C</u>
1	2	3	4	5	6	7	8	9	10	11	12	13	14	15	16
1	1	2	3	5	8	13	21	34	55	89	144	233	377	610	987

3) The sum of any ten numbers in the sequence is divisible by 11.

4) No two consecutive Fibonacci numbers have any common factors.

5) The sum of all Fibonacci numbers in the sequence up to any point, plus 1, equals the Fibonacci number two steps ahead of the last one added.

6) The sum of the squares of any consecutive sequence of Fibonacci numbers beginning at the first 1 will always equal the last number of the sequence chosen times the next higher number.

7) The square of a Fibonacci number minus the square of the second number below it in the sequence is always a Fibonacci number.

8) The square of any Fibonacci number is equal to the number before it in the sequence multiplied by the number after it in the sequence plus or minus 1. The plus and minus 1 alternate along the sequence.

9) One mind-stretching phenomenon, which to our knowledge has not previously been mentioned, is that the ratios between Fibonacci numbers yield numbers which very nearly are thousandths of other Fibonacci numbers with the difference being a thousandth of a third Fibonacci number, all in sequence (see ratio table, Figure 63). Thus, in ascending direction, identical Fibonacci numbers are related by 1.00, or .987 plus .013, adjacent Fibonacci numbers are related by 1.618, or 1.597 plus .021, alternate Fibonacci numbers are related by 2.618, or 2.464 plus .034, and so on. In the descending direction, adjacent Fibonacci numbers are related by .618, or .610 plus .008; alternate Fibonacci numbers are related by .382, or .377 plus .005; second alternates are related by .236, or .233 plus .003; third alternates are related by .146, or .144 plus .002; fourth alternates are related by .090, or .089 plus .001; fifth alternates are related by .056, or .055 plus .001; sixth through twelfth alternates are related by ratios which are themselves thousandths of Fibonacci numbers beginning with .034. It is interesting that by this analysis, the ratio then between thirteenth alternate Fibonacci numbers begins the series back at .001, one thousandth of where it began! On all counts, we have truly a creation of "like from like," of "reproduction in an endless series."

Finally, we note that $(\sqrt{5} + 1)/2 = 1.618$ and $(\sqrt{5} - 1)/2 = .618$, where $\sqrt{5} = 2.236$, an important factor in the Wave Principle and the logarithmic spiral.

1.618 or .618 is known as the Golden Ratio or Golden Mean. Its proportions are pleasing to the eye and an important phenomenon in music, art, architecture and biology. William Hoffer, writing for the December 1975 <u>Smithsonian Magazine</u> (copyright 1975, Smithsonsian

Institution), said:

> ...the proportion of .618034 to 1 is the mathe-
> matical basis for the shape of playing cards
> and the Parthenon, sunflowers and snail shells,
> Greek vases and the spiral galaxies of outer
> space. The Greeks based much of their art and
> architecture upon this proportion. They called
> it "the golden mean."
>
> Fibonacci's abracadabric rabbits pop up in the
> most unexpected places. The numbers are
> unquestionably part of a mystical natural
> harmony that feels good, looks good and even
> sounds good. Music, for example, is based on
> the 8-note octave. On the piano this is
> represented by 8 white keys, 5 black ones -- 13
> in all. It is no accident that the musical
> harmony that seems to give the ear its greatest
> satisfaction is the major [third] . The note E
> vibrates at a ratio of .62500 to the note C. A
> mere .006966 away from the exact golden mean,
> the proportions of the major [third] set off
> good vibrations in the cochlea of the inner ear
> -- an organ that just happens to be shaped in a
> logarithmic spiral.
>
> The continual occurrence of Fibonacci numbers
> and the golden spiral in nature explains
> precisely why the proportion of .618034 to 1 is
> so pleasing in art. Man can see the image of
> life in art that is based on the golden mean.

The Pythagorean brotherhood chose the five-
pointed star as their symbol, as every segment of the
figure is in golden ratio to the next smaller segment.
The ancient Egyptians consciously enshrined forever the
Golden Ratio in the Great Pyramid of Gizeh by giving it
an apothem whose length is 161.8% of half its base, so
that the height of the pyramid is the square root of
161.8% times half its base. According to Peter
Tompkins, author of <u>Secrets of the Great Pyramid</u> (Harper
& Row, 1971), "This relation shows Herodotus' report to
be indeed correct, in that the square of the height of
the pyramid is [the square root of phi times the square
root of phi] = phi, and the areas of the face 1 x phi =
phi." Using these proportions, the Egyptian scientists,
in order to build a scale model of the Northern Hemi-
sphere, used pi and phi in an approach so mathematically

sophisticated that it accomplished the feat of squaring the circle and cubing the sphere, a feat which was not duplicated for over four thousand years. Tompkins explains, "The pharaonic Egyptians, says Schwaller de Lubicz, considered phi not as a number, but as a symbol of the creative function, or of reproduction in an endless series: to them it represented 'the fire of life, the male action of sperm, the logos of the gospel of St. John.'" If man's progress is indeed "reproduction in an endless series," is it not possible that such progress has the form of phi, and that the form is discernable in the movement of the stock market?

The Golden Section

Any length can be divided in such a way that the ratio between the smaller part and the larger part is equivalent to the ratio between the larger part and the whole (see Figure 64). That ratio is always .618.

Figure 64

"Plato, in his _Timaeus_," says Peter Tompkins, "went so far as to consider it, and the resulting Golden Section proportion, the most binding of all mathematical relations, and makes it the key to the physics of the cosmos." In the sixteenth century Johannes Kepler, in writing about the Golden, or "Divine Section," said that it symbolized God's creation of "like from like." In some ways, God may have a hand in the stock market. Is all of mankind's progress a creation of "like from like?"

The Golden Rectangle

The sides of a Golden Rectangle are in the proportion of 1.618 to 1. To construct a Golden Rectangle, start with a square of 2 units by 2 units and draw a line from the mid-point of one side of the square to one of the corners formed by the opposite side as shown in Figure 65.

Triangle EDB is a right-angled triangle.

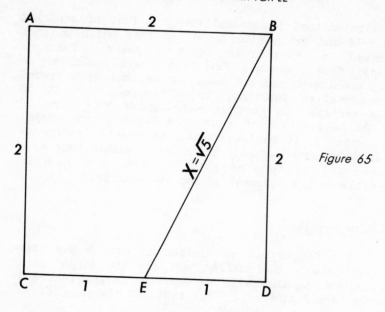

Figure 65

Pythagoras, around 550 B. C., proved geometrically that the square of the hypotenuse of a right-angled triangle equals the sum of the squares of the other two sides. Therefore X squared = 2 squared + 1 squared, or X squared = 5. The length of the line EB, then, must be the square root of 5. The next step in the construction of a Golden Rectangle is to extend the line CD, making EG equal to the square root of 5 or 2.236 units in length, as shown in Figure 66.

When completed, both the rectangle AFCG and BFDG are Golden Rectangles. The proofs are as follows:

$$CG = \sqrt{5} + 1 \qquad \text{and} \qquad DG = \sqrt{5} - 1$$

$$FG = 2 \qquad\qquad\qquad\qquad FG = 2$$

$$\frac{CG}{FG} = \frac{\sqrt{5} + 1}{2} \qquad\qquad \frac{DG}{FG} = \frac{\sqrt{5} - 1}{2}$$

$$= \frac{2.236 + 1}{2} \qquad\qquad = \frac{2.236 - 1}{2}$$

$$= \frac{3.236}{2} \qquad\qquad\qquad = \frac{1.236}{2}$$

$$= 1.618. \qquad\qquad\qquad = .618.$$

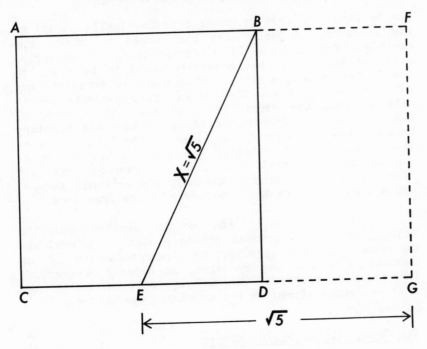

Figure 66

Since the sides of the rectangles are in the proportion of the Golden Ratio, then, the rectangles are, by definition, Golden Rectangles.

Works of art have been greatly enhanced with knowledge of the Golden Rectangle. Leonardo da Vinci, who found the ratio pleasing in its proportions, said, "If a thing does not have the right look it does not work." Many of his paintings had the right look for reasons other than DaVinci's artistic talents, since he used his mathematical knowledge to enhance many of his works using the Golden Ratio. In DaVinci's painting "St. Jerome," he depicts his subject in a crouched position in such a way that a Golden Rectangle can be placed over the figure, containing it perfectly. DaVinci attributed great meaning to the Golden Ratio and took pleasure in its application to artistic works. Other works of art, such as Salvador Dali's "The Sacrament of the Last Supper" utilize many Golden Rectangles.

While it may have been used consciously and deliberately by artists for their own reasons, the phi proportion apparently does have an effect upon the viewer of art. Experimenters have determined that people find the .618 proportion aesthetically pleasing. For instance, subjects have been asked to choose one rectangle from a group of different types of rectangles with the average choice generally found to be close to the Golden Rectangle shape. When asked to cross one bar with another in a way they liked best, subjects generally divided the first one into the phi proportion. Windows, picture frames, buildings, books and cemetery crosses often conform quite close to the Divine Proportion. Another experimenter measured sixty-five women and found their navel height, on the average, was .618 times their total height, divinely proportioned indeed, and a fine symbol of the creation of "like from like."

However, while the Golden Section and the Golden Rectangle represent static pieces of natural and man-made aesthetic beauty, the representation of an aesthetically pleasing dynamism, an orderly progression of growth or progress, can be made only by one of the most remarkable forms in the universe, the Golden Spiral.

The Golden (Logarithmic) Spiral

If we start with a Golden Rectangle, we can take the next step, the construction of the logarithmic spiral. We can draw a large Golden Rectangle, as in

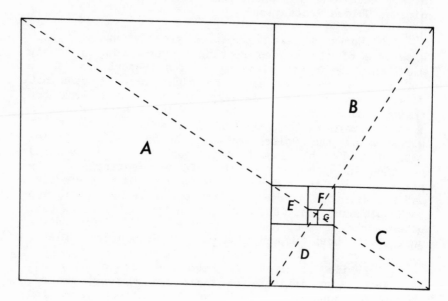

Figure 67

Figure 66, and then divide it into a square and a smaller Golden Rectangle, as shown in Figure 67. This process then theoretically can be continued to infinity. The resulting squares we have drawn, which appear to be whirling inward, are marked A, B, C, D, E, F, and G.

The dotted lines, which are themselves in the golden proportion to each other, diagonally bisect the rectangles and pinpoint the theoretical center of the whirling squares. From this central point, we can draw the spiral as shown in Figure 68 by connecting the points of intersection for each whirling square, in order of increasing size. As the squares whirl inward and outward, their connecting points trace out a logarithmic spiral. The same process, using a sequence of expanding triangles, also can be used to construct a logarithmic spiral.

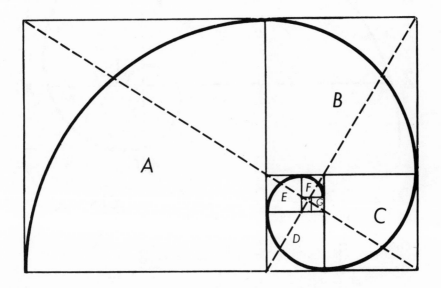

Figure 68

The logarithmic spiral has no boundaries and is a constant shape. The center is never met and the outward reach is unlimited. The core of a logarithmic spiral seen through a microscope has the same look as a spiraling galaxy viewed through a telescope. It is the only spiral that never changes its shape.

At any point in the evolution of a logarithmic

spiral, the ratio of the length of the arc to its
diameter is 1.618. Furthermore, as a study of the
whirling squares reveals, each radius from the
theoretical center of the spiral is 1.618 times as long
as that which precedes it at a 90 degree angle. Each
arc and each diameter is related to its 90 degree
predecessor in the same manner. These relationships,
illustrated in Figure 69, are the building blocks of the
logarithmic spiral. They hold true at every point along
the spiral, and are the reason that the spiral maintains
the same shape, no matter how far "inward" or "outward"
one travels.

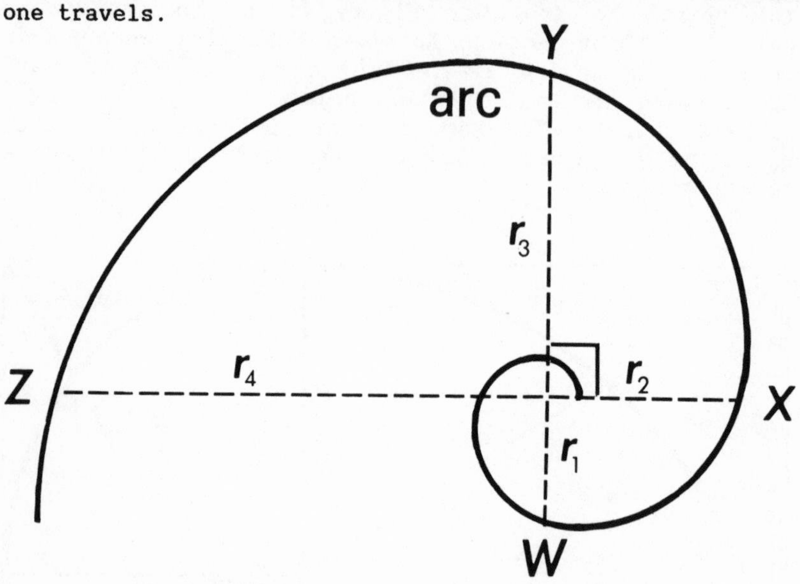

$$\frac{r_2}{r_1} = \frac{r_3}{r_2} = \frac{r_4}{r_3} = \ldots = \frac{r_n}{r_{n-1}} = \underline{1.618}$$

$$\frac{d_2}{d_1} = \frac{d_3}{d_2} = \ldots = \frac{d_n}{d_{n-1}} = \underline{1.618}$$

(where $d_1 = r_1 + r_3$, $d_2 = r_2 + r_4$, etc.)

$$\frac{arcXY}{arcWX} = \frac{arcYZ}{arcXY} \text{, etc.} = \frac{arcXZ}{arcWY} = \underline{1.618}$$

$$\frac{arcWY}{diam. (WY)} = \frac{arcXZ}{diam. (XZ)} \text{, etc.} = \underline{1.618}$$

Figure 69

The logarithmic spiral further indicates that one can go to infinity in a minus quantity from any point in the spiral and one can go to infinity in a plus quantity from the same point. Both ends of the spiral must meet somewhere in infinity in the form of a circle (zero) as there is no other place to meet. Plus and minus quantities must meet somewhere, and added together give zero. Zero is never nothing; it is always something. If we start from zero, we go back to zero. When we multiply zero by infinity we get any given quantity or number, indicating that at any given point some value must exist. Within the progression from ashes to ashes and dust to dust then, there is something which meets the circumstance of awareness. Thus the logarithmic spiral spreads before us in symbolic form, as one of nature's grand designs, the image of life in endless expansion and contraction on the same plane, the within and the without sustained by a common umbilical law: the 1.618 ratio or Golden Mean.

History abounds with examples of learned men who held a special fascination for this particular mathematical formulation. Of course the earliest known, and probably the most interesting, is that of the priests of the Gizeh pyramid of Egypt, who recorded the secret of phi in its construction. Furthermore, it has been reported that the Great Pyramid was used as a temple of initiation for those who proved themselves worthy to understand the great universal secrets. Only those who could rise above the crude acceptance of things as they seemed on the surface to discover what, in actuality, they were, could be instructed in "the mysteries." The stock market, in our opinion, can be understood if it is taken for what it is rather than for what it seems it should be on the surface, that is, as a record of the formal structure of the progress of man rather than a formless mess reacting to current news events.

That the secret of phi was emobodied in the Great Pyramid by the Egyptians as one of the great secrets of the universe was more than the recording of an interesting phenomenon. Learned Egyptians were comfortable with concepts of infinite time and space and of the afterlife. Geometry, astronomy and mathematics were the core of these beliefs. The concept of infinity and of limitless growth is wonderfully represented by the Golden Spiral, as they understood, and by the Elliott Wave Principle, which is built upon the law of the logarithmic spiral. Compare this concept with

astronomer William Kingsland's words in The Great
Pyramid in Fact and in Theory that Egyptian
astronomy/astrology was a "profoundly esoteric science
connected with the great cycles of man's evolution," and
with Madame Blavatsky's words in Isis Unveiled that the
Pyramid "symbolized the creative principle of Nature."
Philosopher Manly P. Hall, who contributed a photograph
to Elliott's Nature's Law, said that the enlightened in
the Pyramid temple learned that "all the universe was
life, all the universe was progress, all the universe
was eternal growth," which is exactly what the Wave
Principle reveals. This realization, he contended,
brought the initiated "to the light of God." For some
then, the "light of God" has been revealed through an
understanding of the principle behind the logarithmic
spiral, a principle of continuous growth and unaltered
form.

        It is this form which gives structure and unity
to the universe. Nothing in nature suggests that life
is disorderly or formless. The word "universe" means
"one order." If life has form, then we must not reject
the probability that the stock market, which is part of
the reality of life, will also have form. All technical
approaches to understanding the stock market depend on
the basic principle of order and form. Elliott's
theory, however, goes beyond all other theories in the
study of form. It postulates that no matter how minute
or how large the form, the basic design remains constant.

        Elliott, in his second monograph, used the
title Nature's Law -- The Secret of the Universe in
preference to "The Wave Principle" and applied it to all
sorts of human activity. Both Pythagoras, who in a
self-portrait held a pyramid marked "The Secret of the
Universe" in his right hand, and Isaac Newton, who had
the logarithmic spiral carved on the headboard of his
bed, would probably have agreed with this formulation.
Our view is that it was a mistake on Elliott's part to
imply that the Wave Principle was the secret of the universe, as nature has created numerous shapes and forms,
not just one simple design. However, it most certainly
would have been credible to say that it was one of the
most important secrets of the universe. Even this
grandiose claim may be only so much tall talk to many
investors, and quite understandably so, as the grand
nature of the concept stretches the imagination and
confounds the intellect. How can Man comprehend a
principle which operates on the same mathematical basis

in the Heavens as it does in the stock market? To illustrate the depth of this question, we must turn to some examples.

As Mr. Bergamini points out, the tail of a comet curves away from the sun in a logarithmic spiral. The epeira spider spins its web into a logarithmic spiral. Bacteria grow at an accelerating rate that can be plotted along a logarithmic spiral. Meteorites, when they rupture the surface of the Earth, cause depressions that correspond to the logarithmic spiral.

Snails, oysters, and other soft-bodied members of the mollusk family have hard shells which grow in the form of a logarithmic spiral in much the same way as the galaxies of outer space expand. In Figures 70 and 71, we see a reflection of the Cosmic Influence in the form of the logarithmic spiral in a snail's shell (drawn by Joan Oman) and in a spiraling galaxy (photo courtesy of Hale Observatories, Pasadena, California). Eons of time and light years of space separate these two formations, but the design is the same: a 1.618 ratio, or in simpler terms, a 5-3 relationship. This circumstance may be nature's way of saying that while in the end time and space are naught, there are, nevertheless, laws governing the ongoing development of the numerous manifestations of natural phenomena.

Elliott himself outlined many more examples of the reflection of the Fibonacci sequence and the Golden

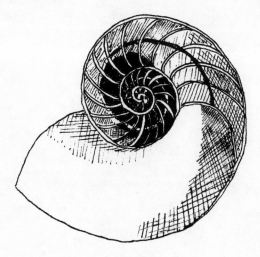

Figure 70

Figure 71

Ratio in natural and human phenomena, including the
dimensions of the Great Pyramid of Gizeh, the arrangement of seed curves on the sunflower, the subdivisions
of a piano keyboard, man's body height, which is divided
at the navel into the Golden Ratio, and the breakdown of
man's limbs: five appendages, three jointed parts to
each appendage (except the head), five digits at the end
of each appendage, and three jointed sections to each
digit (except the big toe). If you're still with us,
the question in your mind is, "Does all this really have
something to do with the stock market?!"

The answer is yes, the stock market has the
very same mathematical base as do these natural phenomena. The idealized Elliott concept of the progression
of the stock market, as presented in Figure 3, Chapter
1, is an excellent base from which to construct the
Golden Spiral, as Figure 72 illustrates with a rough

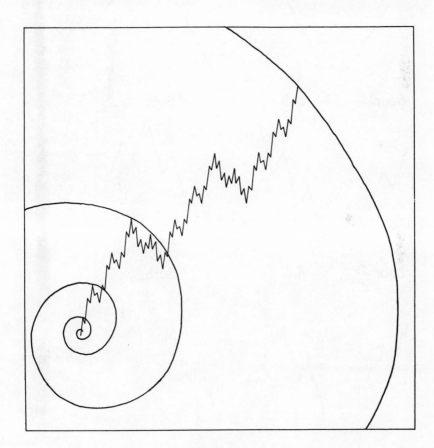

Figure 72

approximation. In this construction, the top of each successive wave of higher degreee is the touch point of the logarithmic expansion.

This result is possible because at any level of stock market activity, a bull market subdivides into five legs and a bear market subdivides into three legs, giving us the 5-3 relationship which is the mathematical basis of the Elliott Wave Principle. We can generate the complete Fibonacci sequence, as we first did in Figure 3, by using Elliott's concept of the progression

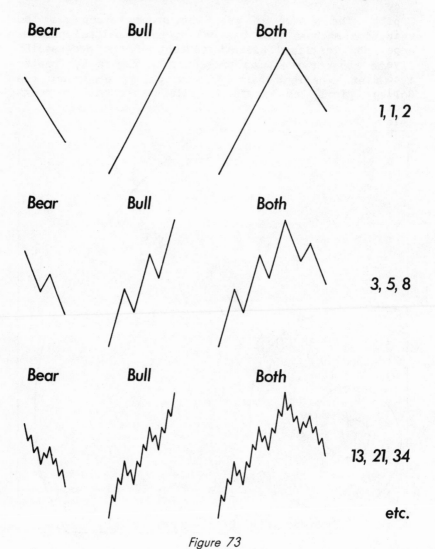

Figure 73

of the market. If we start with the simplest expression of the concept of a bear swing, we get one straight line decline. A bull swing, in its simplest form, is one straight line advance. A complete cycle is two lines. In the next degree of complexity, the corresponding numbers are 3, 5, and 8. As illustrated in Figure 73, this sequence can be taken to infinity.

The stock market's patterns are repetitive in that the same basic pattern of movement which shows up in minor waves, using hourly plots, shows up in Super-cycles and Grand Supercycles, using monthly or yearly plots. Figures 74 and 75 show two charts, one reflect-ing the hourly fluctuations in the Dow over a ten day period from June 25th to July 10th, 1962 and the other a yearly plot of the S & P 500 Index, from 1932 to 1978, courtesy of The Media General Financial Weekly. Both plots indicate similar patterns of movement despite a difference in the time span of over 1500 to 1. The long-term formulation is still unfolding, as wave V from

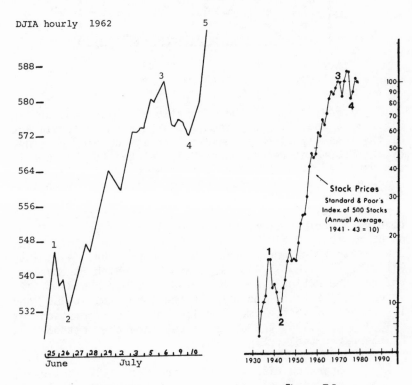

Figure 74   Figure 75

the 1974 low has not run its full course, but to date
the pattern is along lines parallel to the hourly
chart. Why? Because in the stock market, form is not a
slave to the time element. Under Elliott's rules, both
short and long-term plots reflect a 5-3 relationship
which can be aligned with the form contained in the
Fibonacci sequence of numbers. This truth suggests that
man's emotions, in their mass expression, are keyed to a
law of nature.

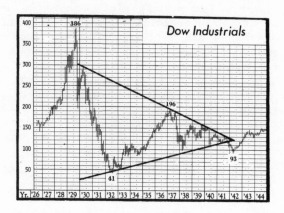

Figure 76

Now compare the formations which appear in
Figures 76 and 77. They each illustrate the natural law
of the inwardly directed Golden Spiral and are governed
by the Fibonacci ratio. Each wave relates to the previous wave by .618. In fact, the distances in terms of
the Dow points themselves reflect Fibonacci mathematics. In the 1930-1942 sequence, the market swings cover
approximately 260, 160, 100, 60, and 38 points respectively, closely resembling the declining list of Fibonacci ratios: 2.618, 1.618, 1.00, .618 and .382. The
Dow levels which mark turning points are 294, 41, 194,
99, 158, (112), 134, 115, 130, and 93, which themselves
reflect the ratios 3.00, .50, 2.00, 1.00, 1.618, (112,
which is .382 times the high of the formation at 296 and
its inverse, 2.618, times the low of the formation at
41), 1.382, 1.146, 1.236, and 1.090 (see the bottom row
of the ratio table, Figure 63).

Starting with wave two in the 1977 triangle,
the swings are almost exactly 55 points (wave Ⓑ), 34
points (wave Ⓒ), 21 points (wave Ⓓ), 13 points
(wave a of Ⓔ) and 8 points (wave b of Ⓔ), the

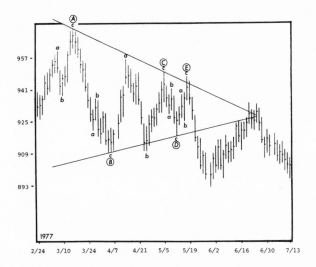

Figure 77

Fibonacci sequence itself. The total net gain from beginning to end is thirteen points and the apex of the triangle lies exactly on the level of its beginning at 930, which is also the level of the peak of the subsequent reflex rally in June. Whether one takes the actual levels and distances of the waves as coincidence or part of the design, one can be certain that the precision manifest in the constant .618 ratio between each successive wave is not coincidence.

   The next figure to consider is Figure 78, a chart, courtesy of Edson Gould and Anametrics, Inc., of the "decennial pattern," as averaged out over the past seven decades in the stock market. In other words, this chart is a reproduction of the DJIA action, since its inception, for the composite decade, years one through ten. The tendency toward similar market action in each year of the decade is well documented and is referred to as the "decennial pattern." Our approach, however, gives this observation a new and startling meaning. Look for yourself: a perfect Elliott Wave.

   To conclude our illustrations in the stock market, take a look at Figure 79, an hourly chart of the most recent market action: the first four minor waves in the DJIA rally off the March 1, 1978 low. The waves are textbook Elliott from beginning to end, from the length of waves to the volume pattern (not shown) to the trend channels to the double retracement of extensions

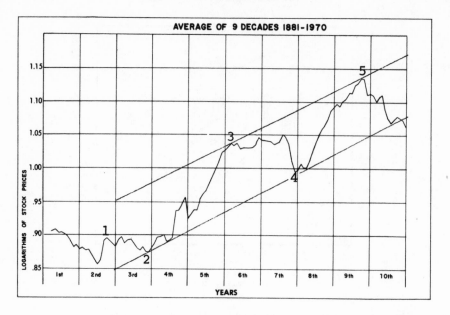

Figure 78

to the expected low for the fourth wave to the perfect
internal counts to the rule of alternation to the Fibonacci time sequences to the Fibonacci ratio relationships embodied within.   It might be worth noting that
914 would be a reasonable target in that it would mark a
.618 retracement of the 1976-1978 decline.

          The spiral-like form of market action is
repeatedly shown to be governed by the Golden Ratio,
and, as you can see, even the Fibonacci numbers
themselves appear in market statistics more often than
mere chance would allow. However, it is crucial to
understand that the numbers themselves have no theoretic
weight in the grand concept of the Wave Principle.   It
is the ratio which is the key to growth patterns of this
type because, although it is rarely pointed out in the
literature, the Fibonacci ratio results from this type
of additive sequence no matter what two numbers start
the sequence. The Fibonacci Sequence is the best known
and most basic additive sequence of its type since it
begins with the number "1" (see Figure 80a). However,
you may also take any two randomly selected numbers such
as 17 and 352 and add them to produce a third, continuing

DJIA Hourly -- 1978

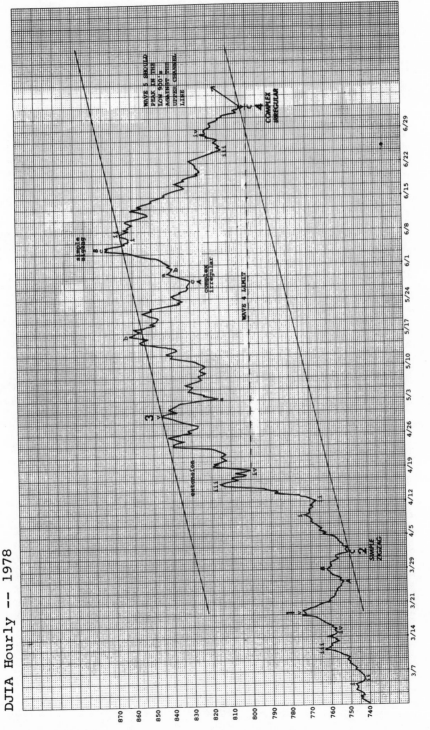

Figure 79

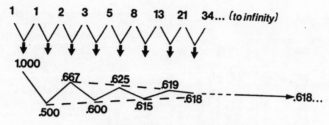

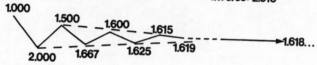

Ratio between alternate numbers: .382
Inverse: 2.618

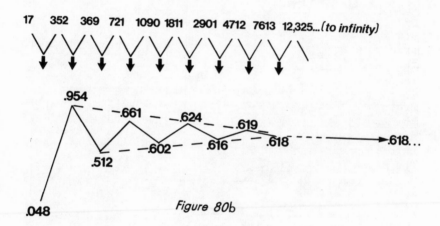

Figure 80a

Figure 80b

in that manner to produce additional numbers. You will find that as this sequence progresses, the ratio between adjacent terms in the sequence will approach the limit phi very quickly. This relationship becomes obvious generally before the tenth term is produced (see Figure 80b). Thus, while specific numbers making up the Fibonacci sequence are not necessarily important in markets, the Fibonacci ratio is a basic law of geometric progression, and does govern many relationships in data series relating to natural phenomena of growth and decay.

In its broadest sense, the Elliott Wave Principle puts forth the proposition that the same law that
shapes the spiraling galaxies of the heavens molds the
spirit and attitudes of man en masse. The Elliott Wave
Principle shows up so clearly in the market because the
stock market is the greatest manifestation of mass
psychology in the world, a nearly perfect reflection of
the mass psychological state of man, intertwined with
the reality of man's progress, the economy and the
business world. Whether our readers accept or reject
this proposition makes no great difference, as the
empirical evidence is available for study and observation. But in our opinion, all these parallels are too
great to be dismissed as just so much nonsense. On the
balance of probabilities, we have come to the conclusion
that there is a Principle, everywhere present, giving
shape to our affairs, and that Einstein knew what he was
talking about when he said, "God does not play dice with
the universe." The stock market is no exception, as
mass behavior is undeniably linked to a law which can be
studied and defined. The briefest way to express this
principle is a simple mathematical statement: the 1.618
ratio.

The Desiderata by poet Max Ehrmann reads:"You
are a child of the Universe, no less than the trees and
the stars; you have a right to be here. And whether or
not it is clear to you, no doubt the Universe is
unfolding as it should." Order in life? Yes. Order in
the stock market? Apparently.

PART II

ELLIOTT APPLIED

In 1939, twelve articles by R. N. Elliott entitled "The Wave Principle" were published. The original publisher's note, in the introduction to the articles, stated the following:

During the past seven or eight years, publishers of financial magazines and organizations in the investment advisory field have been virtually flooded with "systems" for which their proponents have claimed great accuracy in forecasting stock market movements. Some of them appeared to work for a while. It was immediately obvious that others had no value whatever. All have been looked upon by The Financial World with great skepticism. But after investigation of Mr. R. N. Elliott's Wave Principle The Financial World became convinced that a series of articles on this subject would be interesting and instructive to its readers. To the individual reader is left the determination of the value of the Wave Principle as a working tool in market forecasting, but it is believed that it should prove at least a useful check upon conclusions based on economic considerations.

The Editors of The Financial World

In this section, we reverse their suggested procedure and determine that economic considerations may be thought of as an ancillary tool in checking market forecasts based entirely upon the Elliott Wave Principle.

FOUR

RATIO ANALYSIS AND FIBONACCI TIME SEQUENCES

Ratio Analysis

Ratio analysis is the proportionate relationship, in time and amplitude, of one wave to another. In applying the Golden Ratio to the five up and three down movement of the stock market cycle, one might anticipate that on completion of any bull phase the ensuing correction of three waves would be three-fifths of the previous rise in both time and amplitude. Such simplicity, however, is seldom seen but the underlying tendency of the market to conform to the Golden Ratio is always present and helps generate the right look for each wave.

The formulas for calculating what we call time and amplitude ratios are as follows:

$$\frac{\text{Number of points in correction}}{\text{Number of points in advance}} = \text{Amplitude Ratio}$$

$$\frac{\text{Number of time units in correction}}{\text{Number of time units in advance}} = \text{Time Ratio}$$

For general purposes, when either the time or amplitude ratio indicates a sub-normal correction, the undertone of the market is usually quite strong, suggesting that a dynamic thrust may be in the making. Conversely, larger than normal ratios indicate weakness. Beyond this simple application, the study of ratio analysis in the stock market can often lead to such startling discoveries that some Elliott theorists have become almost obsessive about its importance. Years of plotting the averages have convinced the authors that virtually all waves are interrelated, often in several ways, by the ratios between Fibonacci numbers. However, we shall endeavor to present the evidence and let it stand or fall on its own merit.

The first evidence we found of the application of time and amplitude ratios in the stock market comes from, of all suitable sources, the works of the great Dow Theorist, Robert Rhea. In 1936, Rhea, in his book The Story of the Averages, compiled a consolidated summary of market data covering nine Dow Theory bull markets and nine bear markets spanning a thirty-six year time period from 1896 to 1932. He had this to say about why he felt it was necessary to present the data despite the fact that no use for it was immediately apparent:

Whether or not [this review of the averages] has contributed anything to the sum total of financial history, I feel certain that the statistical data presented will save other students many months of work...consequently it seemed best to record all the statistical data we had collected rather than merely that portion which appeared to be useful...the figures presented under this heading probably have little value as a factor in estimating the probable extent of future movements; never-theless, as a part of a general study of the averages, the treatment is worthy of consider-ation.

One of these random observations was this one:

The footings of the tabulation shown above (considering only the industrial average) show that the nine bull and bear markets covered in this review extended over 13,115 calendar days. Bull markets were in progress 8,143 days, while the remaining 4,972 days were in bear markets. The relationship between these figures tends to show that bear markets run 61.1 per cent of the time required for bull periods.

And finally,

Column 1 shows the sum of all primary movements in each bull (or bear) market. It is obvious that such a figure is considerably greater than the net difference between the highest and lowest figures of any bull market. For exam-ple, the bull market discussed in Chapter II started (for Industrials) at 29.64 and ended at 76.04, and the difference, or net advance, was 46.40 points. Now this advance was staged in four primary swings of 14.44, 17.33, 18.97, and 24.48 points respectively. The sum of these advances is 75.22, which is the figure shown in Column 1. If the net advance 46.40 is divided into the sum of advances, 75.22, the result is 1.621, which gives the per cent shown in Column 1. Assume that two traders were infallible in their market operations, and that one bought stocks at the low point of the bull market and retained them until the high day of that market before selling. Call his gain 100 per cent.

Now assume that the other trader bought at the bottom, sold out at the top of each primary swing, and repurchased the same stocks at the bottom of each secondary reaction -- his profit would be <u>162.1</u>, compared with 100 realized by the first trader. Thus the total of secondary reactions retraced <u>62.1</u> per cent of the net advance. [Emphasis added.]

So in 1936 Robert Rhea discovered, without knowing it, the Fibonacci ratio and its function relating bull phases to bear in both time and amplitude. He felt that there is value in presenting data which cannot be immediately utilized for profit, but which might be used to that end at some future date. Similarly, we feel that there is much to learn on the ratio front and our introduction, which merely scratches the surface, could be valuable in leading some future analyst to answer questions we have not even thought to ask.

Besides the Wave Equality guideline (see page 57), ratio analysis has revealed three other ratio relationships which occur more often than not:

1) Wave five is related by the Fibonacci ratio to the net advance from the beginning of wave one to the top of wave three.

2) Wave C is related by a Fibonacci ratio, usually 1.618, to the length of wave A. In some cases, wave C will bottom below the low of wave A by .618 times the length of wave A.

3) The waves of a symmetrical triangle usually are related to each other by .618.

Elliott himself, a few years after Rhea's book, was the first to realize the applicability of ratio analysis. He noted that the number of DJIA points between 1921 and 1926 was 61.8% of the number of points in the last wave from 1926 to 1928 (1928 is the orthodox top of the bull market according to Elliott). Exactly the same relationship occurred again in the five waves up from 1932 to 1937.

Charles J. Collins, in the 1957 Elliott Wave Supplement to the <u>Bank Credit Analyst</u>, gave this price forecast based on expectations of typical wave behavior:

The powerhouse that will be building up if the

> market consolidates for another year or so
> along orthodox lines, it seems to us, will
> offer the probability that Primary V could be
> quite sensational, taking the DJIA to 1000 or
> more [in the early 1960's] in a wave of great
> speculation.

Then, in commenting in <u>The Elliott Wave Principle -- A
Critical Appraisal</u> on the examples cited by Elliott,
Bolton stated,

> Should the 1949 market to date adhere to this
> formula, then the advance from 1949 to 1956
> (361 points in the DJIA) should be completed
> when 583 points (161.8% of 361 points) have
> been added to the 1957 low of 416, or a total
> of 999 DJIA. Alternatively, 361 over 416 would
> call for 777 in the DJIA.

Later, when Bolton wrote the 1964 Elliott Wave Supplement, he concluded:

> Since we are now well past the 777 level, it
> looks as if 1000 in the averages could be our
> next target.

The year 1966 proved those statements to be the
most accurate prediction in stock market history, when
the 3:00 p.m. hourly reading on February 9th registered
a high at 995.82 (the "intraday" high was 1001.11). Six
years prior to the event, then, Bolton was right to
within 3.18 DJIA points, less than one third of one per
cent error.

Despite this remarkable portent, it was
Bolton's view, as it is ours, that wave form analysis
must take precedence over proportionate relationships of
waves in a sequence. Indeed it is sometimes essential
that one understand and apply the Elliott counting and
labeling methods to determine from which points the
measurements should be made in the first place when a
ratio analysis is undertaken.

The authors themselves have used ratio analysis, often with remarkable success. A. J. Frost became
convinced of his ability to recognize turning points by
catching the "Cuban crisis" low in October 1962 the hour
it occurred and telegramming his conclusion to Hamilton
Bolton in Greece. Then, in 1970, in a supplement to <u>The
Bank Credit Analyst</u>, he computed the bear market low for

the Cycle wave correction in progress as likely bottoming at a level .618 times the distance of the 1966-67
decline below the 1967 low, or 572. Four years later,
the DJIA's hourly reading in December 1974 at the exact
low was 572.20, from which the explosive rise into 1975
occurred.

In the summer of 1976, Robert Prechter used the
1.618 ratio to compute the maximum expected low for the
fourth wave expanding triangle in progress to be 922 on
the Dow. The low occurred at 920.63 at 11:00 on November 11th, prior to the fifth wave year-end rally.
Several times during 1977 and early 1978, in published
reports for Merrill Lynch, he used ratio analysis to
pick minor turning points. Then in October 1977, five
months in advance, he computed a probable level for the
1978 major bottom as "744 or slightly lower." On March
first, 1978 at 11:00, the Dow registered exactly
740.30. A follow-up report published two weeks after
the bottom reaffirmed the importance of the 740 level,
noting that:

> ...the 740 area marks the point at which the
> 1977-78 correction, in terms of Dow points, is
> exactly .618 times the length of the entire
> bull market rise from 1974 to 1976. Mathemati-
> cally we can state that 1022 - (1022-572)x.618
> = 744 (or using the orthodox high on December
> 31st, 1005 - (1005-572)x.618 = 737). Secondly,
> the 740 area marks the point at which the
> 1977-78 correction is exactly 2.618 times the
> length of the preceding correction in 1975 from
> July to October, so that 1005 - (885-784)x2.618
> = 742. Thirdly, in relating the target to the
> internal components of the decline, we find
> that the length of wave C = 2.618 times the
> length of wave A if wave C bottoms at 746.
> Even the wave factors as researched in the
> April 1977 report mark 740 as a likely level
> for a turn. At this juncture then, the wave
> count is compelling, the market appears to be
> stabilizing, and the last acceptable Fibonacci
> target level under the Cycle dimension bull
> market thesis has been reached at 740.30 on
> March 1st. It is at such times that the
> market, in Elliott terms, must "make it or
> break it."

> Since the fifth wave of wave C is a diagonal
> triangle which is by nature a weak structure,

it should be swiftly retraced by a rally back to its beginnings at 830-850.

At this point in time, 740.30 seems to be firmly established as the low of Primary wave ② in Cycle wave V.

The 740 level has proved important other times in the past as well, quite possibly because while the 1974 low at 572.20 lies exactly 423.60 points under the 1966 peak at 995.82, 740.30 lies approximately 261.80 points under the 1004.65 level, the orthodox top in 1976. Both of these distances are expressions of Fibonacci ratios. Mr. Prechter discussed the 740 level as follows (see dotted line in Figure 100, Chapter 8):

> It is certainly not coincidence that the 740 level has proved of some importance in the past. In 1961, the intraday Dow peak at 741.30 accompanied the highest market P/E ratio in history; in 1967, the intraday low of 735.74 marked the end of the first slide to the measuring low in the Cycle wave IV bear market (the point which was 61.8% of the entire decline of Cycle wave IV); in 1963, 1970, 1974 and 1975, breaks through 740 in each direction accompanied extreme violence; in 1978, the 740 level corresponds with long-term trendline support. Furthermore, the Wave Principle holds that the limit of any market correction is the bottom of the previous fourth wave of lesser degree. When the first wave in a five-wave sequence extends, however, the limit of the ensuing correction is often the bottom of the second wave of that five-wave sequence. Given this guideline, the recent low on March first at 740.30 was a remarkable level at which to stop. A check with the hourly back figures as printed in the Wall Street Journal reveals that on March 25, 1975 the DJIA bottomed at 740.30 to complete the pullback of the second wave.

In addition to the more traditional Elliott forecasting methods, Mr. Prechter has begun to research mathematical wave factors in terms of both time and price, of which impulse waves have been found to be whole number multiples and corrective waves Fibonacci ratio multiples. The approach was discussed recently in several reports for Merrill Lynch.

Undoubtedly to some it will seem that we are

patting ourselves on the back, which we most certainly
are! Truthfully, though, we are hoping that an account
of the successes which we have personally experienced
with Elliott will inspire others to strive for similar
successes with this approach. To our knowledge, only
the Wave Principle can be used to forecast with such
accuracy. Of course we have experienced failures as
well, but nevertheless we feel that any drawbacks in the
Elliott approach have been grossly overstated in the
past, and that when expectations with regard to the
market are not fulfilled, Elliott Wave Analysis warns
the analyst in plenty of time to chart the next most
likely course and to avoid losses by letting the market
itself dictate his course of action.

We have found that predetermined price objec-
tives are useful in that _if_ a reversal occurs at that
level and the wave count is acceptable, a doubly significant point has been reached. Moreover, it is often
possible, after a minor low has been made which the
Elliott analyst erroneously considers of major importance, to recognize at a higher level that the market is
vulnerable again to new lows. This recognition occurs
after a clear-cut _three_-wave rally follows the minor low
rather than the necessary five, since a three-wave rally
is the symbol of upside weakness in Elliott analysis.
Thus, it is often what happens after the turning point
that helps confirm or refute the assumed status of the
low or high.

If a complete method of ratio analysis could be
successfully resolved into a basic tenet, which does not
appear possible, the Elliott Wave Principle would become
an exact science. Bolton's advice with respect to ratio
analysis was "KEEP IT SIMPLE." Fortunately it is possible to delve into the finer points of ratio analysis and
at the same time follow Bolton's dictum. The ratios
which we have found to be important in the market are
always the simplest ones. The more complicated task of
the analyst is to discover which waves in the past and
future are related to the others in this manner.
Research may still achieve further progress, as ratio
analysis is still in its infancy. We are confident that
E. A. Hollingsworth of Maryland, Dr. C. R. Wiley of
Florida and others who have labored with the problem of
ratio analysis will add worthwhile material to the
Elliott approach.

The ratio problem is a mathematical problem.
Einstein again went to the crux of the situation when he

said, "As far as the laws of mathematics refer to reality they are not certain and as far as they are certain they do not refer to reality." Mathematics is not likely to reduce the problem of ratio analysis inherent in the Wave Principle to a science any more than in any other area of human endeavor but that does not say that progress cannot be made. All that can be said about ratio analysis at this point is that comparing waves frequently confirms, often with pinpoint accuracy, the applicability of the ratios found in the Fibonacci sequence to the stock market. It was awe-inspiring, but no surprise to us, for instance, that the advance from December 1974 to July 1975 traced just over 61.8% of the preceding 1973-74 bear slide, or that the 1976-78 market decline traced exactly 61.8% of the preceding rise from December 1974 to September 1976. Despite the continual evidence of the importance of the .618 ratio, our basic reliance must be on <u>form</u>, with ratio analysis as back-up or guideline to what we see in the patterns of movement.

Time Sequences

Time is not a predictable property of the Wave Principle in terms of fixed periodicity and consequently there is no sure way of using the time factor by itself in forecasting. Frequently, however, time sequences based on the Fibonacci series go beyond an exercise in numerology and seem to fit wave spans with remarkable accuracy, giving the analyst added perspective. Elliott said that the time factor often "conforms to the pattern" and therein lies its significance. In wave analysis, time periods often serve to indicate possible turning areas, especially if their durations coincide with price targets and wave counts.

In <u>Nature's Law</u>, Elliott gave the following examples of Fibonacci time spans between important turning points in the market (see Chapter 5, Figure 78):

1921 to 1929	8 years
July 1921 to November 1928	89 months
September 1929 to July 1932	34 months
July 1932 to July 1933	13 months
July 1933 to July 1934	13 months
July 1934 to March 1937	34 months
July 1932 to March 1937	5 years (55 months)
March 1937 to March 1938	13 months
March 1937 to April 1942	5 years
1929 to 1942	13 years

In the <u>Dow Theory Letter</u> dated November 21, 1973, Richard Russell gives some additional interesting examples of time periods which appear beyond coincidence:

1907 panic low to 1962 panic low	55 years
1949 major bottom to 1962 panic low	13 years
1921 depression low to 1942 depression low	21 years
January, 1960 top to October 1962 bottom	34 months

Walter E. White, in his 1968 monograph on the Elliott Wave Principle, concluded that "the next important low point may be in 1970." As substantiation, he pointed out the following Fibonacci series: 1949 + 21 = 1970; 1957 + 13 = 1970; 1962 + 8 = 1970; 1965 + 5 = 1970. May 1970, of course, marked the low point of one of the most vicious slides in market history.

The progression of years from the 1928 (possible orthodox) and 1929 (nominal) high of the last Supercycle produces a remarkable Fibonacci sequence:

1929 + 3 = 1932 bear market bottom
1929 + 5 = 1934 correction bottom
1929 + 8 = 1937 bull market top
1929 + 13 = 1942 bear market bottom
1928 + 21 = 1949 bear market bottom
1928 + 34 = 1962 crash bottom
1928 + 55 = 1983 probable Supercycle peak

A similar series has begun at the 1965 (possible orthodox) and 1966 (nominal) highs of the third Cycle wave of the current Supercycle:

1965 + 1 = 1966 nominal high
1965 + 2 = 1967 reaction low
1965 + 3 = 1968 blowoff peak for secondaries
1965 + 5 = 1970 crash low
1966 + 8 = 1974 bear market bottom
1966 + 13 = 1979 low for 9.2 and 4.5 year cycles
1966 + 21 = 1987 probable Supercycle low

Thus, we foresee some interesting possibilities with respect to DJIA turning points in the near future. These possibilities are further explored in the last chapter.

In applying Fibonacci time periods to the pattern of the market, Bolton noted that time "permutations tend to become infinite" and that time "periods will produce tops to bottoms, tops to tops, bottoms to bottoms or bottoms to tops." Despite this reservation, he successfully indicated within the same book, which was published in 1960, that 1962 or 1963, based on the Fibonacci sequence, could produce an important turning point. 1962, as we now know, did produce a vicious bear market and a low which preceded one of the longest uninterrupted primary advances in history.

In addition to this type of time sequence analysis, the time relationship between bull and bear as discovered by Robert Rhea has proved useful in forecasting. Robert Prechter, in writing for Merrill Lynch, noted in March 1978 that "April 17 marks the day on which the A-B-C decline would consume 1931 trading hours, or .618 times the 3124 trading hours in the advance of waves (1), (2) and (3)." Friday, April 14 marked the upside breakout from the dull inverse head and shoulders pattern on the Dow and Monday, April 17 was the explosive day of record volume, 63.5 million shares, showing that Fibonacci had picked the exact day when the pressure of the bear was off the market.

Benner's Theory

In 1875, Samuel T. Benner, an Ohio wheat farmer, wrote a rather interesting book entitled Business Prophecies of the Future Ups and Downs in Prices. The forecasts contained in this book are based mainly on cycles in pig-iron prices and the recurrence of financial panics over a fairly considerable period of years. Benner, prior to becoming a farmer and a part-time statistician, had been an iron-works manufacturer. The post Civil War panic of 1873 ruined him financially so he turned to farming and took up the study of price movements as a hobby to find, if possible, the answer to the recurring ups and downs in business. Mr. Benner's forecasts proved remarkably accurate for many years and he established an enviable record for himself as a statistician and forecaster. Even today, Benner's charts are of interest to students of cycles and are occasionally seen in print, sometimes without due credit to the originator.

Benner noted that the highs of business tend to follow a repeating 8-9-10 yearly pattern. If we apply this pattern to high points in the Dow-Jones Industrial Average over the past seventy-five years starting with 1902, we get the following results:

| | YEARLY | |
YEAR	INTERVAL	MARKET HIGHS
1902		April 24, 1902
1910	8	January 2, 1910
1919	9	November 3, 1919
1929	10	September 3, 1929
1937	8	March 10, 1937
1946	9	May 29, 1946
1956	10	April 6, 1956
1964	8	February 4, 1965
1973	9	January 11, 1973

The dates are not projections based on Benner's forecasts from earlier years, but are only an application of the 8-9-10 repeating pattern applied in retrospect. The fit is satisfactory, but whether the pattern will always reflect the future highs is another question.

With respect to economic low points, Benner noted two series of time sequences indicating that recessions (bad times) and depressions (panics) tend to alternate (not surprising, given Elliott's rule of alternation). In commenting on panics, Benner observed that 1819, 1837, 1857, and 1873 were panic years and showed them in his original "panic" chart to reflect a repeating 16-18-20 pattern, resulting in an irregular periodicity of these recurring events. Although he applied a 20-18-16 series to recessions, or "bad times," less serious stock market lows seem rather to follow the same 16-18-20 pattern as do major panic lows. Thus by applying the 16-18-20 series to the alternating stock market lows, we again get a surprisingly accurate fit, as the Benner-Fibonacci Cycle Chart (Figure 81), first published in the 1967 supplement to the Bank Credit Analyst, graphically illustrates.

Note that the last time the time-cycle configuration was the same as the present was the period of the 1920's, paralleling both the Kondratieff picture, which we discuss in Chapter 7, and the last occurrence of a fifth Elliott wave of Cycle dimension.

While it is unwarranted to ascribe great predictive value to Benner's repeating series for tops and bottoms, the formula has worked reasonably well for most of this century, so we give some credence to it. In our search for the reason, we find that the basis of Benner's theory conforms reasonably closely to the Fibonacci sequence, in that the repeating series of 8-9-10

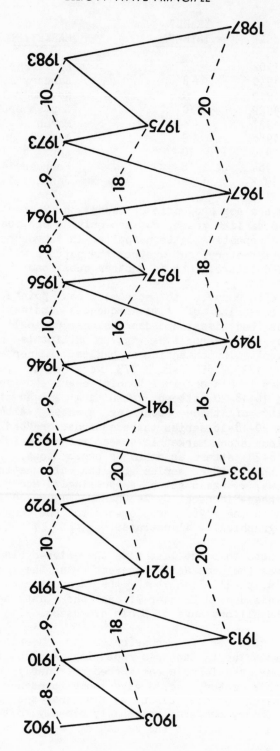

The Benner–Fibonacci Cycle Chart 1902–1987

PEAKS: 8–9–10, repeat. TROUGHS:16–18–20,repeat. MAJOR TROUGHS:16–18–20,repeat.

Figure 81

produces Fibonacci numbers up to number 337, allowing for a marginal difference of one point, as follows:

8-9-10 SERIES	SELECTED SUBTOTALS	FIBONACCI NUMBERS	DIFFERENCES
8	8	8	0
9			
10			
8	35	34	+1
9			
10	54	55	-1
8	89	89	0
9			
10			
8	143	144	-1
9	233	233	0
10	378	377	+1

Our conclusion is that Benner's theory, which is based on different rotating time periods for bottoms and tops rather than constant repetitive periodicities, falls within the framework of the Fibonacci sequence and thus within the framework of one of Nature's laws. Had we no experience with the approach, we might have treated it with less emphasis, but it has proved remarkably useful in the past when used in conjunction with a knowledge of Elliott Wave progression. A. J. Frost applied Benner's concept in 1964 to make the inconceivable (at the time) prediction that stock prices were doomed to move essentially sideways for the next ten years, reaching a high in 1973 at about 1000 DJIA and a low in the 500 to 600 zone in late 1974 or early 1975. In a letter sent to Hamilton Bolton at the time, Frost wrote as follows:

December 10, 1964

Mr. A. H. Bolton
Bolton, Tremblay, & Co.
1245 Sherbrooke Street West
Montreal 25, Quebec

Dear Hammy:

Now that we are well along in the current period of economic expansion and gradually becoming vulnerable to changes in investment sentiment, it seems prudent to polish the crystal ball and do a little hard assessing.

In appraising trends, I have every confidence in your
bank credit approach except when the atmosphere becomes
rarefied. I cannot forget 1962. My feeling is that all
fundamental tools are for the most part low pressure
instruments. Elliott, on the other hand, although
difficult in its practical application, does have
special merit in high areas. For this reason I have
kept my eye cocked on the Wave Principle and what I see
now causes me some concern. As I read Elliott, the

Frost's view of
Elliott in prospect.

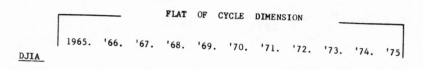

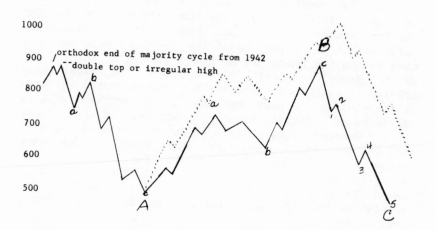

NOTES:

a) Elliott's theory of alternation calls for a FLAT of major or
cycle dimension comprised of the next three primaries. The
last major bear market 1929-42 appears to be on an upward
zig-zag.

b) Massive monetary stimulation would likely give the above
pattern an upward and forward tilt as indicated by dotted
line

c) Wave 3 extension from June 1949 to January 1960 (post war
bull market) of cycle wave from 1942 should not be violated
to any great extent. The downward limit therefore should
not be too far off 500.

d) Benner's rules of fixed periodicity have been applied to
primary tops and bottoms - marked A, B & C.

Figure 82

stock market is vulnerable and the end of the major cycle from 1942 is upon us.

...I shall present my case to the effect that we are on dangerous ground and that a prudent investment policy (if one can use a dignified word to express undignified action) would be to fly to the nearest broker's office and throw everything to the winds.

The third wave of the long rise from 1942, namely June 1949 to January 1960, represents an extension of primary cycles....then the entire cycle from 1942 may have reached its orthodox culmination point and what lies ahead of us now is probably a double top and a long flat of cycle dimension.

...applying Elliott's theory of alternation, the next three primary moves should form a flat of considerable duration. It will be interesting to see if this develops. In the meantime, I don't mind going out on the proverbial limb and making a 10-year projection as an Elliott theorist using only Elliott and Benner ideas. No self-respecting analyst other than an Elliott man would do such a thing, but then that is the sort of thing this unique theory inspires.

Best to you,

A. J. Frost

In Figure 82 we have repoduced the chart which Frost enclosed in his letter to Hamilton Bolton, complete with notes. As the letter was dated December 10, 1964, it represents yet another long-term Elliott prediction which turned out to be more fact than fancy.

Application of the Fibonacci ratios to the stock market can be approached from many angles. The more one studies the Wave Principle, the more perceptive his analyses should become. By no means has the Elliott approach been researched thoroughly enough to say that no doors are left to be opened with this magnificent key. The approaches suggested here are merely carrots to whet the appetite of prospective analysts and set them on the right track. Parts of the following chapters further explore the use of ratio analysis and give perspective on its complexity, accuracy and applicability. The key is there. All that remains is to discover how many doors it will unlock.

FIVE

LONG TERM WAVES AND AN UP-TO-DATE COMPOSITE

Forbes (September 15, 1977) published an interesting article on the complexity theory of inflation
entitled "The Great Hamburger Paradox," in which the
writer, David Warsh, asks, "What really goes into the
price of a hamburger? Why do prices explode for a
century or more and then level off?" He quotes Professor E. H. Phelps Brown and Sheila V. Hopkins of Oxford
University as saying:

> For a century or more, it seems, prices will
> obey one all-powerful law: it changes and a
> new law prevails; a war that would have cast
> the trend up to new heights in one dispensation
> is powerless to deflect it in another. Do we
> yet know what are the factors that set this
> stamp on an age; and why, after they have held
> on so long through such shakings, they give way
> quickly and completely to others?

Brown and Hopkins state that prices seem to
"obey one all-powerful law," which is exactly what R. N.
Elliott said. This so-called all-powerful law is the
harmonious relationship found in the Fibonacci sequence
of numbers, the Golden Ratio, the Golden Section, the
Golden Rectangle, the Golden Spiral and nature. Because
this harmonious relationship is part of nature's law, it
works itself into the fabric of man's emotional
structure as an impelling force. As Mr. Warsh argues in
"The Great Hamburger Paradox," human progress seems to
move in sudden jerks and jolts, not as in the smooth
clockwork operation of Newtonian physics. We agree with
Mr. Warsh's conclusion but further posit that these
shocks are not of only one noticeable degree of metamor-
phosis or age, but occur at all degrees along the logarithmic spiral of man's progress and the progress of the
universe, from minuette degree and smaller to Grand
Supercycle degree and greater. And to introduce another
paradox, we suggest that these shocks themselves are
part of the clockwork. A watch may appear to run
smoothly, but its progress is controlled by the
spasmodic jerks of a timing mechanism, whether mechanical or quartz crystal. Quite likely the logarithmic
spiral of universal progress is propelled in exactly the
same manner.

If you say "nuts" to this thesis, please
consider that we are not talking about a compelling

force, but an impelling one. Any rejection of the Wave Principle as an exogenous impelling law of nature leaves unanswered the questions, "How? Why?" to which there is no satisfactory answer based on empirics. All we want is to demonstrate that there is a force or law which generates form in the market averages, despite the fundamental prejudices and pretentiously posited theoretical economic models we all encountered in textbooks.

We suppose the average investor has little interest in what may happen to his investments when he is dead or what the investment environment of his great-great-great-great grandfather was. It is difficult enough to cope with current conditions in the daily battle for investment survival without concerning ourselves with the distant future or the long-buried past. However, long-term wave perspectives cannot be entirely ignored, first because the developments of the past serve greatly to determine the future, and secondly because it can be illustrated that the same law that applies to the long term applies to the short term and produces the same patterns of stock market behavior.

In this chapter we shall outline the current position of the progression of "jerks and jolts" from what we call the Millennium Cycle wave to today's Primary wave bull market. Moreover, as we shall see, because of the position of the Millennium Cycle wave and the pyramiding of "fives" in our final composite wave picture, this decade could prove to be one of the most exciting times in world history to be writing about and studying the Elliott Wave Principle.

1. The Millennium Cycle Wave from the Dark Ages

For the last two hundred years, data available for researching price trends is not especially difficult to attain, but prior to that time we have to rely on less exact statistics for perspective. The long-term price index compiled by Professor E. H. Phelps Brown and Sheila V. Hopkins and further enlarged by David Warsh (taken from "The Great Hamburger Paradox," which appeared in Forbes magazine, September 15, 1977), is based on a simple "market basket of human needs" for the period from 950 A.D. to 1954.

By splicing the price curves of Brown and Hopkins onto industrial stock prices from 1789, we get a long-term "Millennium" picture of prices for the last

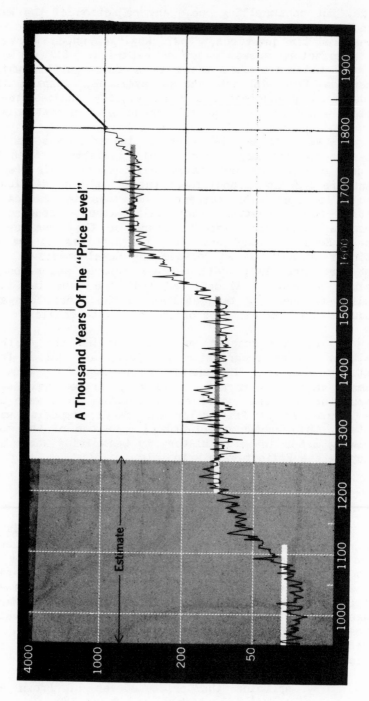

A Thousand Years Of The "Price Level"

Figure 83

one thousand years. Figure 83 shows approximate general
price swings from the Dark Ages to 1789. For the fifth
wave from 1789 we have overlaid a straight line to
represent stock price swings in particular, which we
will analyze further in the next section. Strangely
enough this diagram, while only a very rough indication
of price trends, produces an unmistakable Elliott
pattern.

Paralleling the broad price movements of
history are the great periods of commercial and industrial expansion over the centuries. Rome, whose great
culture at one time may have coincided with the peak of
the previous Millennium Cycle wave, finally fell in 476
A.D. and for five hundred years afterward the search for
knowledge became almost extinct. The Commercial Revolution (950-1350), eventually sparked the first new Grand
Supercycle wave of expansion that ushered in the Middle
Ages. The leveling of prices from 1350 to 1520 forms
wave two and represents a "correction" of the progress
during the Commercial Revolution.

The second period of rising prices, the third
Grand Supercycle wave, coincides with both the Capitalist Revolution (1520-1640) and with the greatest period
in English history, the Elizabethan period. Elizabeth I
(1533-1603) came to the throne of England just after an
exhausting war with France and soon became the dominant
personality of her time. The country was poor and in
despair, but before Elizabeth died, England had defied
all the powers of Europe, expanded her empire and become
the most prosperous nation of the world. This was the
age of Shakespeare, Martin Luther, Drake and Raleigh,
truly a glorious epoch in world history. Business
expanded and prices rose during this period of pomp,
brilliance and luxury, the likes of which may not be
seen again until the next occurrence of a Millennium
Cycle's third wave. By 1650, prices had reached a peak,
leveling off to form Grand Supercyle wave four.

The fifth Grand Supercycle wave within this
Millennium Cycle wave appears to begin for commodity
prices around 1760 rather than our presumed time period
for the stock market around 1770 to 1790, which we have
labeled "1789" where the stock market data begins.
However, as a study by Gertrude Shirk in the April/May
1977 issue of Cycles magazine points out, trends in
commodity prices have tended to precede similar trends
in stock prices generally by about a decade. Viewed in
light of this knowledge, the two measurements actually
fit together extremely well. This last great up-wave of

the Millennium Cycle coincides with the burst in produc-
tivity generated by the Industrial Revolution (1750-
1850) and parallels the rise of the United States of
America as a world power.

Elliott logic suggests that the Grand Supercycle from 1789 to date must both follow and precede
other cycles bearing some relationship in time and
amplitude. If this be true, then the 1000-year Millennium Cycle wave, unless it is extending, has almost run
its full course and stands to be corrected by three
Grand Supercycles (two down and one up), which could
extend over the next five hundred years. It is difficult to think of a no-growth situation in world econo-
mies lasting for such a long period but the possibility
cannot be ruled out. The broad hint of long-term
trouble, of course, does not necessarily preclude the
possibility of sound management, common sense and the
growth in technology mitigating the severity of what
might be presumed to develop. The Elliott Wave Principle is a law of probability and relative degree, not a
law of inevitability. The end of the current Supercycle
V, which we expect in about 1983, could coincide with
some form of economic or social shock ushering in
another era of decline and despair. After all, if it
was the Barbarians who finally toppled a rotting Rome,
can it be said that the modern day Barbarians do not
have adequate means and a similar purpose?

2. The Grand Supercycle Wave from 1789 to the Present

This long wave has the right look of three
waves in the direction of the main trend and two against
the trend for a total of five, complete with an extended
third wave corresponding with the most dynamic and
progressive period of U.S. history. In figure 84, the
Supercycle subdivisions have been marked (I), (II),
(III), (IV) and (V).

Considering that we are moving back in market
history to the days of canal companies, horse-drawn
barges and meager statistics, it is surprising that the
record of "constant dollar" industrial share prices,
which was developed by Gertrude Shirk for Cycles magazine, forms such a clear Elliott pattern. Especially
striking is the near perfection of the Elliott trend
channel, the baseline of which connects several important Cycle and Supercycle wave lows and the upper parallel the peaks of several advancing waves. A market high
in 1983 would touch the upper parallel reasonably within

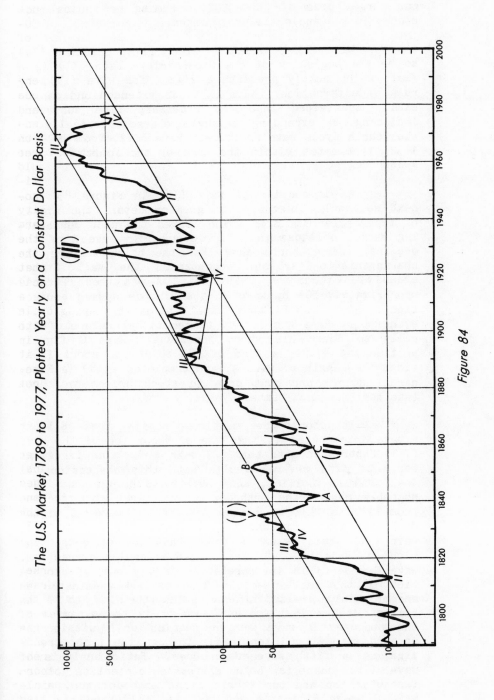

The U.S. Market, 1789 to 1977, Plotted Yearly on a Constant Dollar Basis

Figure 84

our target area of 2500-3000, assuming no radical net change in the wholesale price index.

Wave (I) is a fairly clear five, assuming 1789 to be the beginning of the Supercycle. Wave (II) is a flat, which neatly predicts a zigzag for wave (IV), by rule of alternation. Wave (III) is extended and can be easily subdivided into the necessary five subwaves, including an expanding triangle characteristically in the fourth Cycle wave position. Wave (IV), from 1929 to 1932, terminates within the area of the fourth wave of lesser degree.

An inspection of wave (IV) in Figure 85 (see next section) illustrates in greater detail the zigzag of Supercycle dimension which marked the most devastating market collapse in U.S. history. In wave A of the decline, daily charts show that the third subwave, in characteristic fashion, accompanied the Wall Street crash of October 29, 1929. Wave A was then retraced approximately 50% by wave B, the "famous upward correction of 1930," as Richard Russell terms it, during which even Robert Rhea was led by the emotional nature of the rally to cover his short positions. Wave C finally bottomed at 41.22, a drop of 253 points or about 1.382 times the length of wave A, and completed an 89 (a Fibonacci number) per cent drop in stock prices in three (another Fibonacci number) years.

It should be mentioned again that Elliott always interpreted 1928 as the orthodox top of the wave (III) Supercycle with the 1929 peak marking an irregular top. We find several faults with this contention, as does Charles Collins, who agrees with us that 1929 probably marked the orthodox high. First, the decline from 1929 to 1932 is a fine specimen of a 5-3-5 zigzag decline. Next, for wave (III) to have topped in 1928, wave (IV) would assume a shape that is not consistent with the "right look" for a 3-3-5 irregular correction. Wave C under this interpretation is way out of proportion to the smaller A and B waves and terminates an uncomfortably great distance below the low of A as Elliott counts it. Another problem is the dynamism of the supposed B wave, which remains well within the uptrend channel and terminates through the upper trendline, as a fifth wave often does. Ratio analysis of wave (IV) supports both Elliott's contention of an irregular top and our thesis of an orthodox top, since wave C under Elliott's analysis is 2.618 times as long as the net decline of wave A from November 1928 to

November 1929, and under our analysis wave C is 1.382 times as long as wave A from September 1929 to November 1929, where .382 is the inverse of 2.618.

Wave (V) of this Grand Supercycle is still in progress, but has so far conformed beautifully to the expectation that since wave (III) was an extension, wave (V) should be approximately equal to wave (I) in terms of time and percentage magnitude. Wave (I) took about fifty years to complete, as should wave (V) if it ends in 1983 as we expect. Its height on the constant dollar chart is about equal to the height of wave (V), expressing equality in terms of percentage advance. Even their "looks" are not dissimilar. Wave (V) of the Grand Supercycle is further analysed below.

3. The Supercycle Wave from 1932

This Supercycle wave has been in progress since 1932 and is still unfolding (see Figure 85). If there were such a thing as a perfect wave formation under the Wave Principle, this long-term sequence of Elliott waves would be a prime candidate. The breakdown of Cycle waves is as follows:

Wave I: 1932 to 1937 -- This wave is a clear-cut five-wave sequence according to the rules established by Elliott. It retraces .618 of the market decline from the 1928 and 1930 highs and, within it, the extended fifth wave travels 1.618 times the distance of the first through third waves.

Wave II: 1937 to 1942 -- Within wave II, subwave ⓐ is a five, and wave ⓒ is a five, so the entire formation is a zigzag. Most of the price damage occurs in wave ⓐ . Thus there is great strength in the structure of the entire corrective wave, much beyond what we would normally expect, as wave ⓒ travels only slightly into new low ground for the correction. Most of the damage of wave ⓒ was time based or erosive, as continued deflation pushed stock prices to price/earnings levels which were below those even in 1932. A wave of this construction, however, can have the power of a flat.

Wave III: 1942 to 1965(6) -- This wave must be one of the longest extended Cycle wave

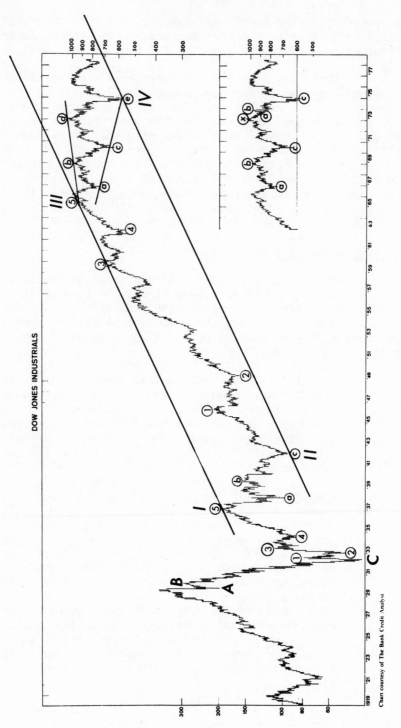

DOW JONES INDUSTRIALS

Figure 85

Chart courtesy of The Bank Credit Analyst

structures in the history of markets. Its principal features are:

1) The market rose over eight hundred per cent in twenty-two years.
2) Wave ④ is a flat, alternating with a zigzag, wave ②.
3) Wave ③ is the longest Primary wave, and itself is an extension.
4) All waves are rhythmic and hug their basic trendlines.
5) Wave ④ corrects to the top zone of the preceding fourth wave of lesser degree and holds well above the peak of wave ①.
6) Wave (c) of wave ④ ends in a failure as the Cuban crisis orthodox low of 554 DJIA in October 1962 holds above the nominal June low of 524.
7) The length of subwaves ① and ⑤ are related by the Fibonacci ratio in terms of percentage advance (129% and 80% respectively, where 80 = 129 x .618) as is often the case between two non-extended waves.

Wave IV: 1965(6) to 1974 -- In Figure 85, two possible interpretations are shown: a five-wave expanding triangle from February 1965 and a double three from January 1966. Both counts are admissible and have the same technical significance, calling for a thrust to the upper parallel line of the trend channel. The triangle interpretation, however, might suggest a lower objective, where wave V would trace an advance approximately as long as the widest part of the triangle. No other Elliott evidence, however, suggests that such a weak wave is in the making. Some Elliott theorists attempt to count the last leg as a five, thus labeling Cycle wave IV a large flat. Our technical objections to a five-wave count of the last move down from January 1973 to December 1974 are mainly that the supposed third subwave is too short and the first wave is then overlapped by the fourth, thereby offending two of Elliott's basic rules.

Wave V: 1974 to 198? -- This wave of Cycle degree is still unfolding. It is likely that two Primary waves have been completed at this juncture and the market is in the process of

tracing out the third Primary, which should
accompany a breakout to new all-time highs.
The last chapter will cover in somewhat more
detail our analysis and expectations with
respect to the current market.

Thus, as we read Elliott, the current bull
market in stocks is the fifth wave from 1932 of the
fifth wave from 1789 of possibly even the fifth wave
from the Dark Ages. Figure 86 gives the composite
picture, and speaks for itself.

Elliott Waves in Descending Magnitude

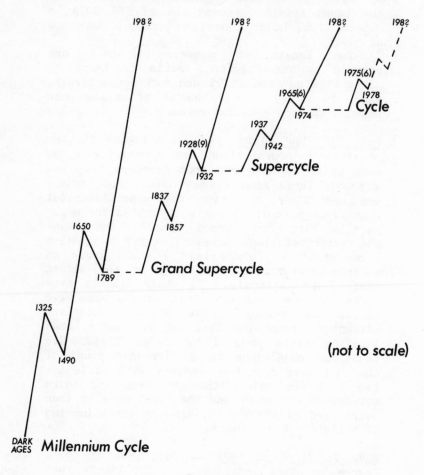

Figure 86

History from the Dark Ages has traced what in retrospect appears to have been an almost uninterrupted phase of human progress. Before this phase, the building of Stonehenge, the rise of the Greek city-states and the expansion of the Roman Empire may have corresponded with Millennium Cycle waves or even upward "corrections" within Millennium Cycle wave declines.

Of course in the theory of the logarithmic spiral, there exist waves of larger degree than Millennium. For instance, the wave of social development which crested at the building of the Great Pyramid after thousands of years of progress in Egypt might be one degree larger than Millennium, say Supermillennium. The ages in the development of the species of Homo sapiens might be referred to as waves of Epochal degree. Perhaps man himself is one stage in the development of even larger waves in the progress of life on Earth. After all, if the existence of the planet Earth is conceived to have lasted so far one year, life forms have been with us for about five weeks, while manlike creatures have walked the Earth for only the last six hours of the year, less than one one-hundredth of the total period during which forms of life have existed. To put these time periods in perspective, we should note that on this basis Rome dominated the Western world for a total of five seconds. Viewed from this perspective, a Millennium Cycle isn't really of such large degree after all.

SIX

STOCKS AND COMMODITIES

Individual Stocks

The art of managing investments is the art of acquiring and disposing of stocks and other securities so as to maximize gains. When to make a move in the investment field is more important than what issue to trade. Stock selection is of secondary importance compared to timing. It is relatively easy to select sound stocks in essential industries if that is what one is after, but the question always to be weighed is when to buy it. To be a winner in the stock market, either as a trader or as an investor, one must know the direction of the primary trend and proceed to invest with it, not against it, in stocks that historically have tended to move in unison with the market as a whole. Fundamentals alone are seldom a proper justification for investing in stocks. U.S. Steel in 1929 was selling at $260 a share and was considered a sound investment for widows and orphans. The dividend was $8.00 a share. The Wall Street crash reduced the price to $22 a share and the company did not pay a dividend for four years. The stock market is usually a bull or a bear, seldom a cow.

Somehow the market averages develop trends which unfold in Elliott Wave patterns regardless of the price movements of individual stocks. While the Wave Principle has some application to individual stocks, as we shall illustrate, the count for many issues is often too fuzzy to be of great practical value. In other words, Elliott will tell you if the track is fast but not which horse is going to win. For the most part, basic textbook technical analysis with regard to individual stocks is probably more rewarding than trying to force the stock's price action into an Elliott count that may or may not exist.

There is reason to this. The Elliott philosophy broadly allows for individual attitudes and circumstances to affect price patterns of any single issue and, to a lesser degree, a narrow group of stocks, simply because what the Elliott Wave Principle reflects is only that part of each man's decision process which is shared by the mass of investors. In the larger reflection of wave form then, the unique circumstances of individual investors and individual companies cancel each other out, leaving as residue a mirror of the mass mind alone. In other words, the form of the Wave

Principle reflects the progress not of each man but of
mankind as a whole and man's investments.   Companies
come and go. Trends, fads, cultures, needs and desires
ebb and flow with the human condition.   Therefore the
progress of general business activity is well reflected
by the Wave Principle, while each individual area of
activity has its own essence, its own life expectancy
and a set of forces which may relate to it alone.   Thus
each stock, like each man, appears on the scene as part
of the whole, plays its part and eventually returns to
the dust from which it came.

        If, through a microscope, we were to observe a
tiny droplet of water, its individuality might be quite
evident in terms of size, color, shape, density, salin-
ity, bacteria count, etc., but when that droplet is part
of a wave in the ocean, it becomes swept along with the
force of the waves and the tides, despite its individuality. With over twenty million droplets owning stocks
listed on the New York Stock Exchange, is it any wonder
that the market averages are one of the greatest manifestations of mass psychology in the world?

        Despite this important distinction, many stocks
tend to move more or less in harmony with the general
market. It has been shown that on average seventy-five
per cent of all stocks move up with the market and
ninety per cent of all stocks move down with the market,
although price movements of individual stocks are usually more erratic than the averages.   Closed-end stocks
of investment companies and stocks of large cyclical
corporations, for obvious reasons, tend to conform to
the patterns of the DJIA more closely than most other
stocks. The best approach seems to be to avoid trying
to analyze each issue on an Elliott basis unless a
clear, unmistakable Elliott pattern unfolds before your
eyes and commands attention.   Decisive action should
best be taken only then, but it should be taken, regardless of the wave count for the market as a whole.
Ignoring such a pattern is always more dangerous than
paying the insurance premium.

        The seven individual stocks shown in Figures
87a through 87g show Elliott Wave patterns, although
each is slightly different. The bull markets for U.S.
Steel, Dow Chemical and Medusa show primary five-wave
advances from their major bear market lows.   Eastman
Kodak and Tandy show A-B-C bear markets into 1978.   The
charts of K Mart (formerly Kresge) and Houston Oil and
Minerals illustrate long-term "growth" type advances

Figure 87a

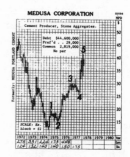

Figure 87b

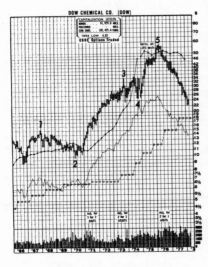

Figure 87c

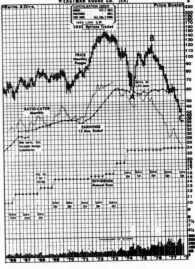

Figure 87d

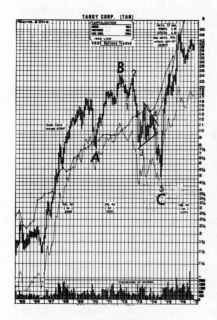

Figure 87e

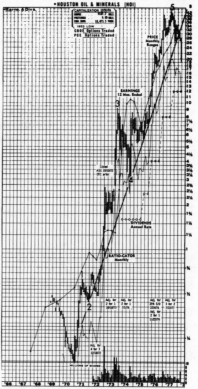

Figure 87f

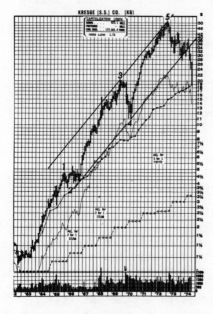

Figure 87g

which trace out Elliott patterns and break their long-term supporting channel lines only after completing satisfactory wave counts.

Commodities

        Commodities have as much individual character as stocks. The difference between commodity charts and charts of the market averages is that in commodities bull and bear markets at times can overlap each other as they are not allowed to in the basic Elliott pattern. Sometimes, for instance, a complete five-wave bull market will fail to take the commodity to a new all-time high, as the chart on soybean futures illustrates (Figure 89). Therefore it seems that the peak observable degree in commodity swings, depending upon the commodity, is usually the Primary or Cycle degree. Beyond this degree, the Principle gets bent here and there. The best Elliott patterns are born from important long-term breakouts from extended sideways base patterns, as occurred in coffee, soybeans, sugar, gold and silver at different times in the 1970's. Unfortunately semi-logarithmic charts, which may have indicated applicability of Elliott trend channels, were not available for this study.

        Figure 88 shows the progress of the two-year price explosion in coffee from mid-1975 to mid-1977. The pattern is unmistakably Elliott, even down to minor wave degree. The ratio analysis employed beautifully predicts the price level not far above which the ultimate high occurs. In this computation, the length of the rise to the peak of wave (3) at $113, multiplied by 1.618 gives $183, which when added to the wave (4) low projects a peak at $303. After the peak of the fifth wave is reached, a devastating bear market strikes apparently out of the blue.

        Figure 89 displays five years of price history for soybeans. The initial explosive rise in 1972-73 came off a long base, as did the explosion in coffee prices. The target area is met beautifully here as well, where the length of the rise to the peak of wave 3, at $4.00, multiplied by 1.618, gives $6.47, which when added to the wave 4 low projects a peak at $11.77. In the ensuing A-B-C bear market, a perfect Elliott zigzag unfolds, bottoming in January 1976. Wave B of this correction is .618 times the length of wave A. A new bull market takes place in 1976-77, although of

COFFEE

NEAR

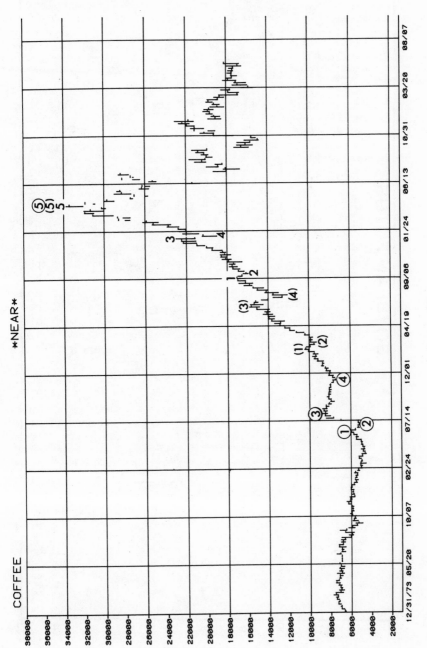

Figure 88

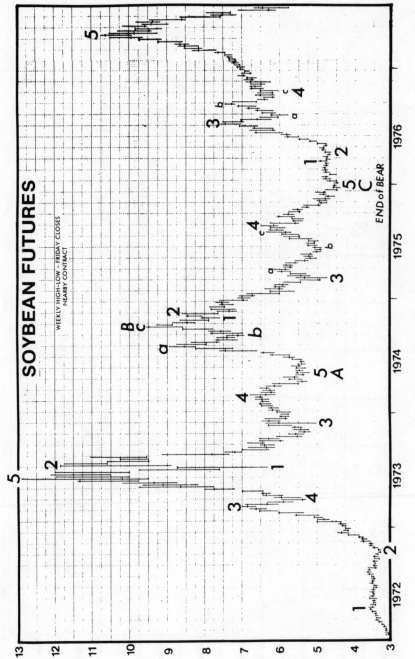

Figure 89

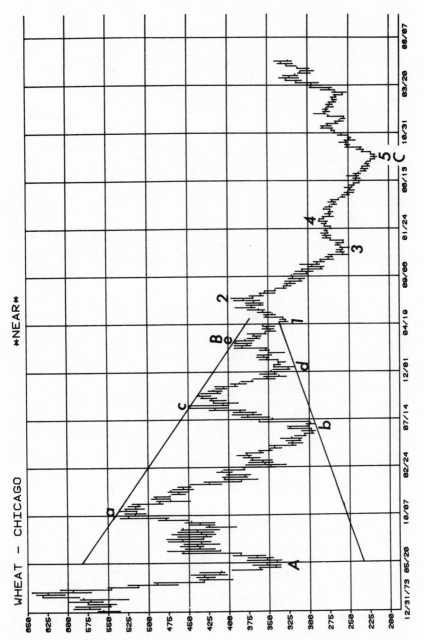

Figure 90

subnormal extent since the peak of wave 5 falls just
short of the expected minimum target of $10.90. The
same computational method is used in this projection as
well, where the gain to the peak of wave 3, at $3.20,
times 1.618 gives $5.20, which when added to the lows
within wave 4 at $5.70, gives the $10.90 target.

Figure 90 is a weekly high-low chart of Chicago
wheat futures. The entire four-year span from the peak
at $6.45 is an Elliott A-B-C bear market with phenomenal
internal interrelationships. Wave B is a symmetrical
triangle exactly like that discussed in Chapter 3.
Again the five touch points conform perfectly with the
boundaries of the trendlines. Again the subwaves
develop as a reflection of the Golden Spiral, with each
leg related to its predecessor by the Fibonacci ratio
after the first downswing. Again the "false breakout"
occurs at the end of the progression, although this time
it is accomplished by wave 2 of C. In addition, the
wave A decline is not only 1.618 times the length of the
first rebound within wave B, but is also approximately
1.618 times as long as wave C.

Thus we can demonstrate that commodities have
properties which reflect the universal order that
Elliott discovered. It seems reasonable to expect,
though, that the more individual the personality of a
commodity, which is to say, the less it is a necessary
part of human existence, the less it will reliably
reflect an Elliott pattern. One commodity that is unal-
terably tied to the psyche of mass humanity is gold.

Gold

Gold often moves "contra-cyclically" to the
stock market. When the price of gold reverses to the
upside after a downtrend it can often occur concurrently
with a turn for the worse in the stocks, and vice
versa. Therefore, an Elliott reading of the gold price
has in the recent past provided confirming evidence for
an expected intermediate turn in the Dow.

In April of 1972, the long-standing "official"
price of gold was increased from $35 an ounce to $38 an
ounce and in February of 1973 was again increased to
$42.22. The fixed official price established by central
banks for convertibility purposes and the rising trend
in the unofficial price in the early seventies led to
what was called the "two-tier" system. In November 1973

the official price and the two-tier system were abolished by the inevitable workings of supply and demand in the free market.

The free market price of gold rose from $35 in January 1970 and reached a London market closing price peak of $197 an ounce on December 30, 1974. The price then started to slide and on August 31, 1976 reached a low of $103.50. The fundamental "reasons" given for this decline have always been U.S.S.R. gold sales, U.S. Treasury gold sales and I.M.F. auctions. Since then the price of gold has recovered substantially and is trending upward again.

Despite the efforts of the U.S. Treasury to diminish gold's monetary role and the highly charged emotional factors affecting gold as a store of value and a medium of exchange, its price has followed an inescapably clear Elliott pattern. Figure 91 is a price chart of London gold and on it we have indicated the correct wave count, in which the point where the free market took off to the peak at $179.50 an ounce on April 3rd, 1974 is a completed five-wave sequence. The officially maintained price of $35 an ounce before 1970 prevented any wave formation prior to that time and thus helped create the necessary long-term base. The dynamic breakout from that base fits well the criterion for the clearest Elliott count for a commodity, and clear it is.

The rocketing five-wave advance forms a nearly perfect wave, with the fifth terminating well against the upper boundary of the trend channel. The usual target projection method is not fulfilled here, although we do find that the $90 rise to the peak of wave III still provides the basis for measuring the distance to the orthodox top, so that $90 x .618 = $55.62, which when added to the peak of wave III at $125, gives $180.62. The actual price at wave V's peak was $179.50, quite close indeed. Also noteworthy is that at $179.50, the price of gold had multiplied by just over five (a Fibonacci number) times its price at $35.

Then in December 1974, after the initial wave A decline, the price of gold rose to an all-time high of nearly $200 an ounce. This wave was wave B of a large irregular correction, which crawled upward along the lower channel line, as corrective wave advances often do. As befits the personality of a "B" wave, the phoniness of the advance was unmistakable. First, the news background, as <u>everyone</u> <u>knew</u>, appeared to be bullish for

London Gold Bullion

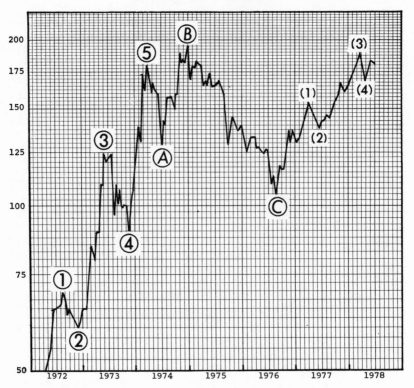

Figure 91

gold, with American legalization of ownership due on January first, 1975. Wave B, in perverse manner, peaked precisely on the last day of 1974. Secondly, gold mining stocks, both North American and South African, were noticeably underperforming on the advance, forewarning of trouble by refusing to confirm the assumed bullish picture.

Wave C, a devastating collapse, accompanied a severe decline in the valuation of gold stocks, carrying some back to where they had begun their advances in 1970. In terms of the bullion price, the authors computed in early 1976 by the usual relationship that the low should occur at about $98, since the length of wave A at $51, times 1.618, equals $82, which when

subtracted from the orthodox high at $180, gives a
target at $98. Note also that the nominal high at $200
minus twice wave A's $51 also equals $98, and that $200
times ½ gives $100, where ½ and 2 are inverses of the
ratio between the Fibonacci numbers 1 and 2. The low
for the correction was well within the zone of the
previous fourth wave of lesser degree and quite close to
the target, hitting $103.50 on August 25, 1976, the
month just between the Dow Theory stock market peak in
July and the nominal DJIA peak in September.

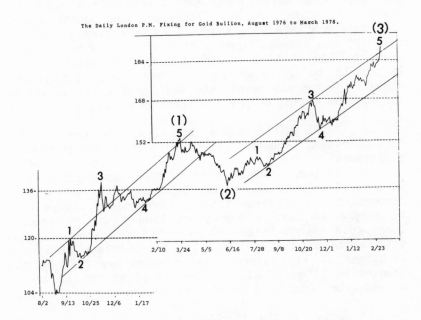

Figure 92

The ensuing advance so far has traced out four
complete Elliott waves and entered a fifth, which should
push the gold price to new all-time highs. Figure 92
gives a near term picture of the first three waves up
from the August 1976 bottom, where each impulse wave
divides clearly into Elliott's five-wave sequences.
Each upward wave also conforms to an Elliott trend
channel on semi-log chart paper. The slope of the rise
is not as steep as the initial bull market advance,
which was a one-time explosion following years of price
control. The current rise seems mostly to be reflecting
the decline in the value of the dollar since in terms of
other currencies gold is not nearly as close to its all-
time high.

Since the price of gold has held the previous fourth wave level on a normal pullback, the count could be a nearly completed five wave sequence or a developing third wave extension, suggesting coming hyperinflationary conditions under which both the stock market and commodities climb together, although we offer no definite opinions on the subject. If this be true, however, the A-B-C irregular correction implies great thrust in the next wave into new high ground. It should be remembered, though, that commodities can form contained bull markets, ones which need not develop into waves of higher and higher degree. Therefore one cannot assume that gold has entered a giant third wave from the low at $35. If the advance forms a distinct five-wave sequence from the low at $103.50 adhering to all Elliott rules, it should be regarded as at least an interim sell signal. Under all cases, the $98 level still should be the maximum extent of any important decline.

Gold, historically speaking, is one of the disciplines of economic life, with a sound record of achievement. It has nothing more to offer the world than discipline. Perhaps that is the reason politicians work tirelessly to ignore it, denounce it and attempt to demonetize it. Somehow though, governments always seem to manage to have a supply on hand "just in case." Today gold stands in the wings of international finance as a relic of the old days but nevertheless also as a harbinger of the future. The disciplined life is the productive life and that concept applies to all levels of endeavor, from dirt farming to international finance.

Gold is the time-honored store of value and, although the price of gold may flatten for a long period, it is always good insurance to own some until the world's monetary system is intelligently restructured, a development which seems inevitable, whether it happens by design or through natural economic forces. That paper is no substitute for gold as a store of value is probably another of nature's laws.

SEVEN

OTHER APPROACHES TO THE STOCK MARKET AND THEIR RELATIONSHIP TO THE WAVE PRINCIPLE

Dow Theory

According to Charles H. Dow's thinking, the primary trend is the broad, all-engulfing "tide" of the market, which is interrupted by the "waves," or secondary reactions and rallies. Movements of lesser degree, the "ripples" on the waves, are generally unimportant unless a line (defined as a sideways structure lasting at least three weeks and contained within a price range of five per cent) is formed. The main tools of the theory were the Rail Average (now the Transportation Average) and the Industrial Average. The leading exponents of Dow's theory, William Peter Hamilton, Robert Rhea, Richard Russell and E. George Schaefer rounded out Dow's theory but never altered his basic tenets.

The Dow Theory is essentially a wave theory based on the concept of similarity of action between the movement of the sea and the trends of the market. As Charles Dow once observed, stakes can be driven into the sands of the seashore as the waters ebb and flow to mark the direction of the tide in much the same way as charts are used to show how prices are moving. Out of experience came the fundamental Dow Theory tenet that, since both averages are part of the same ocean, the tidal action of one average must move in unison with the other to be authentic. Hence the theory of confirmation of action.

The Elliott Wave Principle, apart from the confirmation principle, has points in common with Dow Theory. During impulse waves, the market should be a "healthy" one, with breadth and the other averages confirming the action. When corrective waves are in progress, divergences, or non-confirmations, are likely. Dow's followers also recognized three psychological "phases" of a market advance, which are essentially the same as the personalities of Elliott's three impulse waves as we have outlined them in Chapter 2.

The Wave Principle validates much of Dow Theory but of course Dow Theory does not validate the Wave Principle since Elliott's concept of wave action has a mathematical base, needs only one market average for interpretation and unfolds according to a basic rhythm

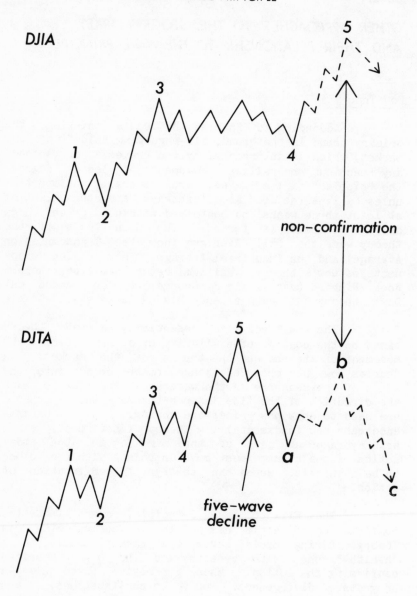

Figure 93

or pattern. Both theories, however, are based on empirical observations and complement each other in theory
and practice. Often, for instance, the Elliott count
can forewarn the Dow Theorist of an upcoming non-
confirmation. If, as Figure 93 shows, the Industrial
Average has completed four waves of a primary swing and
part of a fifth, while the Transportation Average is

rallying in a "B" wave of a zigzag correction, a
non-confirmation is inevitable. In fact, this type of
development has helped the authors more than once. As
an example, in May of 1977, when the Transportation
Average was climbing to new highs, the preceding
five-wave decline in the Industrials during January and
February signaled loud and clear that any rally in that
index would be doomed to non-confirmation.

On the other side of the coin, a Dow Theory
non-confirmation can often alert the Elliott theorist to
examine his count to see whether or not a reversal
should be the expected event. Thus knowledge of one
approach can complement application of the other. Since
Dow Theory is the grandfather of the Wave Principle, it
deserves great respect for its historical significance
as well as its consistent record of performance over the
years.

The Kondratieff Wave

The fifty to fifty-four year cycle of catastro-
phe and renewal had been known and observed by the Mayas
of Central America and independently by the ancient
Israelites. The modern expression of this cycle is the
"long wave" of economic and social trends observed in
the 1920's by Nikolai Kondratieff, a Russian economist.
Kondratieff documented, with the limited data available,
that economic cycles of modern capitalist countries tend
to follow a long rhythmic pattern of approximately half
a century. These cycles parallel in some respects
Elliott's Supercycles.

Figure 94, courtesy of The Media General
Financial Weekly, shows the idealized concept of
Kondratieff waves from the 1780's to the year 2000 and
their relationship to wholesale prices. Notice that the
beginning of wave (I) of the Grand Supercycle shown on
page 125 in Figure 84 to the deep low of wave A of (II)
in 1842 roughly tracks one Kondratieff wave in length,
the extended wave (III) and wave (IV) track most of two
Kondratieffs, and our current Supercycle wave (V) will
last throughout most of one Kondratieff.

Kondratieff noted that "trough" wars usually
occur at a time when the economy stands to benefit from
the price stimulation generated by a war economy,
resulting in economic recovery and an advance in
prices. "Peak" wars, on the other hand, usually occur

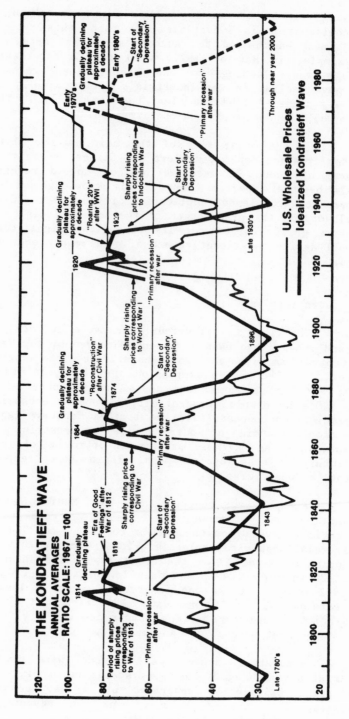

Figure 94

when recovery is well advanced and as the government
pays for the war by the usual means of inflating the
money supply, prices rise sharply. After the economic
peak, a primary recession occurs, which is then followed
by a "plateau" of about ten years' duration in which
relatively stable and prosperous times return. The
aftermath of this period is a severe depression followed
by several years of deflation.

The first Kondratieff wave for the U.S. began
at the trough with the Revolutionary War, peaked with
the War of 1812, and was followed by a plateau period
called the "Era of Good Feeling," which preceded the
depression of the 1830's and '40's. As James Shuman and
David Rosenau describe in their book The Kondratieff
Wave, waves unfolded economically and sociologically in
a surprisingly similar manner throughout the second and
third cycles, with the second plateau accompanying the
Reconstruction period after the War Between the States
and the third aptly referred to as the Roaring Twenties,
which followed World War I. The plateau periods generally supported good stock markets, especially the
plateau period of the 1920's. The roaring stock market
was followed ultimately by collapse, the Great Depression and general deflation until about 1942.

As we interpret the Kondratieff cycle, we have
now reached another plateau, having had a trough war
(World War II), a peak war (Vietnam) and a primary
recession (1974-75). This plateau should again be
accompanied by relatively prosperous times and a strong
bull market in stocks. According to a reading of the
Wave, the economy should collapse in the mid 1980's, and
be followed by three or four years of severe depression
and a long period of deflation through to the trough
year 2000 A.D. This scenario fits ours like a glove and
would correspond to our fifth Cycle wave advance and the
next Supercycle decline, as we discussed in Chapter 5
and further outline in the last chapter.

Cycles

In the 1971 edition of his book Cycles, Edward
R. Dewey states that in a 1965 computer search for
cycles in stock market prices, he had discovered hints
of thirty-seven possible cycles ranging from 2.5 years
to nearly 111 years in duration. This is a long period
to cover in any stock market analysis but in terms of
the spiral-like wave form of the stock market, the

period from 0 to 2.5 years is infinitely greater.

The "cycle" approach to the stock market has become quite fashionable in the past several years, coinciding with the publishing of several books on the subject. Such approaches have a great deal of validity and in the hands of an artful analyst, can be an excellent approach to market analysis. But in our opinion, while it can make money in the stock market as can many other technical tools, the "cycle" approach does not reflect the true essence of the law behind the progression of markets.

Unfortunately, just as the Elliott Wave Principle in conjunction with Dow Theory and one or two related methods spawned a large public following for the "all bull markets have three legs" thesis, the cycle theories have recently spawned a rigid adherence to the "four and a half year cycle" idea by many analysts and investors. Some comments seem appropriate. First, the existence of any cycle does not mean that moves to new highs within the second half of the cycle are impossible. The measurement is always low to low, regardless of intervening market action. Secondly, while the four and a half year cycle has been visible for the post-war period (about thirty years), evidence of its existence prior to that time is spotty and irregular, revealing a history that will allow for its contraction, expansion or disappearance at any time, despite the "presidential cycle" arguments to the contrary.

For those who have found success using a flexible cycle approach, we feel that the Wave Principle can be quite a useful tool in predicting changes in the lengths of cycles, which seem to fade in and out of existence at times, usually with little or no warning. Note, for instance, that the four and a half year cycle has been quite visible in most of the current Supercycle's subwaves II, III, and IV but becomes muddled and distorted in wave I, the 1932-1937 bull market, and prior to that time. If we remember that the two shorter waves in a five-wave bull move tend to be quite similar, we can deduce that the current Cycle wave V should more closely resemble wave I (1932-37) than any other wave in this sequence, since wave III from 1942 to 1966 was the extended wave and will be dissimilar to the other impulse waves. The current wave V, then, should be a simpler structure with shorter cycle lengths and could provide for the sudden contraction of the popular four and a half year cycle to more like three and a half years. In other words, <u>within</u> waves, cycles may tend toward time constancy. When the next wave begins, however, the analyst should be on the alert for changes in periodicity. Since we believe that the debacle currently predicted for 1978 and 1979 by the cycle theorists on the basis of the four and nine year cycles will not occur, we would like to present the following quotation from "Elliott's Wave Principle -- A Reappraisal" by Charles J. Collins, published in 1954 by Bolton, Tremblay & Co.:

> Elliott alone among the cycle theorists (despite the fact he died in 1947, while others lived) provided a basic background of cycle theory compatible with what actually happened in the post-war period (at least to date).
>
> According to orthodox cycle approaches, the years 1951-1953 were to produce somewhat of a holocaust in the securities and commodity markets, with depression centering in this period. That the pattern did not work out as anticipated is probably a good thing, as it is quite doubtful if the free world could have survived a decline which was scheduled to be almost as devastating as 1929-32.
>
> In our opinion, the analyst could go on indefinitely in his attempt to verify fixed cycle periodicities with negligible results. By comparison, the Wave Principle is a simple authentic approach to stock market behavior and needs no computer.

"The News Makes the Market"

While most financial news writers explain market action by current events, there is seldom any worthwhile connection. Most days contain a plethora of both good and bad news, which is usually selectively scrutinized to come up with a plausible explanation for the movement of the market. In <u>Nature's Law</u>, Elliott commented on the value of news as follows:

> At best, news is the tardy recognition of forces that have already been at work for some time and is startling only to those unaware of the trend. The futility in relying on anyone's ability to interpret the value of any single news item in terms of the stock market has long

been recognized by experienced and successful
traders. No single news item or series of
developments can be regarded as the underlying
cause of any sustained trend. In fact, over a
long period of time the same events have had
widely different effects because trend conditions were dissimilar. This statement can be
verified by casual study of the 45 year record
of the Dow Jones Industrial Average.

During that period kings have been assassi-
nated, there have been wars, rumors of wars,
booms, panics, bankruptcies, New Era, New Deal,
"trust busting," and all sorts of historic and
emotional developments. Yet all bull markets
acted in the same way, and likewise all bear
markets evinced similar characteristics that
controlled and measured the response of the
market to any type of news as well as the
extent and proportions of the component
segments of the trend as a whole. These
characteristics can be appraised and used to
forecast future action of the market, regardless of news.

There are times when something totally unexpected happens, such as earthquakes. Nevertheless, regardless of the degree of surprise, it
seems safe to conclude that any such development is discounted very quickly and without
reversing the indicated trend under way before
the event. Those who regard news as the cause
of market trends would probably have better
luck gambling at race tracks than in relying on
their ability to guess correctly the significance of outstanding news items. Therefore the
only way to "see the forest clearly" is to take
a position above the surrounding trees.

Elliott recognized that not news, but something
else forms the patterns evident in the market. Generally speaking, the important question is not the news
per se, but the importance the market places or appears
to place on the news. In periods of optimism, the reaction to an item of news is often different from what it
would be if the market were in a state of collapse. It
is easy to label the progression of Elliott waves on a
historical price chart but it is impossible to pick out,
say, the occurrences of war on the basis of recorded
stock market action. The psychology of the market in

relation to the news is what really counts, especially
when the market acts contrary to what one would normally
expect.

The market, when it is related to the news at
all, discounts the future. During first waves of a bull
market, the market "sees" a better future despite the
gloom spread on the front page of the newspaper. In
third and fifth waves, increasingly good news is part of
the progression of events. As the fifth wave of the
market peaks, a change in the future is sensed, although
the fundamental background tends to remain rosy for
awhile, since the good news tends to peak out well after
the market does. In a sense, we can say that the first
wave of improving fundamentals occurs during the
market's wave "3", the third wave during the market's
wave "5", and the fifth as wave "B" of the market's
corrective process is under way. After the decline, the
fundamental situation has generally seen the worst as
wave "2" of the market's next advance bottoms out. This
parallel progression of events is a sign of unity in
human affairs and tends to confirm the Wave Principle as
an integral part of the human experience. The market
actually informs us in advance of possible changes in
the social condition. To sum up our view, then, the
market essentially is the news.

The Random Walk Theory

The Random Walk Theory has been developed by
statisticians in the academic world. The theory holds
that stock prices move at random and not in accord with
predictable patterns of behavior. On this basis, stock
market analysis is pointless as nothing can be gained
from studying trends, patterns, or the inherent strength
or weakness of individual securities.

An indication of how far this theory is removed
from reality is the chart of the first 89 days of
trading over the New York Stock Exchange after the 740
low on March first, 1978. As shown in Figure 80, the
wave is textbook Elliott from the very beginning. The
Principle is fulfilled from the length of waves to the
volume pattern (not shown) to the trend channels to the
perfect internal counts to the equality of waves to the
double retracement of extensions to the personality of
waves to the limits of corrections to the rule of alternation to the Fibonacci ratio relationships and time
periods embodied within. As this chart illustrates

again, the N.Y.S.E. is never a formless jumble wandering
without rhyme or reason. For 89 consecutive days, the
DJIA indicates price changes that create a succession of
waves dividing and subdividing into patterns which
perfectly fit Elliott's basic tenets as he laid them out
forty years ago. Statistically speaking, this is an
incredible performance, proving that the forces which
animate wave progression are not random or due solely to
chance. It is tantamount to tossing a coin eighty-nine
times in a row with the coin falling "heads" each time.
David Bergamini, in LIFE Science Library/Mathematics
(published by Time-Life Books, Inc.), stated:

> Tossing a coin is an exercise in probability
> theory which everyone has tried: calling
> either heads or tails is a fair bet because the
> chance of either result is one half. No one
> expects a coin to fall heads once in every two
> tosses, but in a large number of tosses the
> results tend to even out. For a coin to fall
> heads fifty consecutive times in a row would
> take a million men tossing coins ten times a
> minute for forty hours a week -- and then it
> would only happen once every nine centuries.

Under the Wave Principle, every market decision
has some meaning. Each transaction winds itself into
the fabric of the market and so enters the chain of
causes which generate form. As form is repetitive at
all levels and for all periods of time, it has predictive value -- a five followed by a three forms a
completed cycle. A completed cycle in the general
context of wave formation tells a story of what to
expect, either with respect to the balance of the
current cycle or the next cycle of higher degree.

Sometimes the market displays a dream-like
quality, but at other times one can see that it reflects
the hard facts of life. Because of this inconsistency,
we must assume that the market has a logic all its own,
a logic which is emphatically not the straight-line
variety one becomes accustomed to in the every day
experiences of life, or even the cyclically rhythmic
machine that some declare it to be. It is a form logic,
a logic of structure. Because of this fact, neophytes
find it difficult to understand the strange, "unreason-
able," sometimes drastic, seemingly random ways of the
market. Thus, as the reader of this book may witness,
the Elliott Wave Principle challenges the Random Walk
Theory at every turn.

Technical Analysis

The Elliott Wave Principle not only proves the validity of chart analysis, but it can help the technician decide which formations are most likely of real significance. As in the Wave Principle, technical analysis recognizes the "triangle" formation as generally an intra-trend phenomenon. The concept of a "wedge" is the same as that for Elliott's diagonal triangle, and has the same implications. "Rectangles" are usually double or triple threes. The famous "head and shoulders" pattern can be discerned in a normal Elliott top (see Figure 95), while a head and shoulders pattern which "doesn't work out" might have been an irregular correction under Elliott (see Figure 96).

Note that in both patterns, the volume characteristics that are expected to accompany the head and shoulders formation are those which are most compatible with the Wave Principle. In Figure 95, wave 3 will have the heaviest volume, wave 5 somewhat lighter, and wave b usually lighter still where the wave is of intermediate degree or lower. In Figure 96, the impulse wave 1 will have the highest volume, wave b usually somewhat less, and wave four of c the least.

Flags and pennants are zigzags and triangles of minute and minuette degree. Double tops are generally caused by flats, double bottoms by failures. Trendlines and trend channels are used similarly in both approaches. Support and resistance phenomena are evident in normal wave progression (the peak of wave one is support for wave four) and in the expectable limits of bear markets. High volume and volatility (gaps) are recognized characteristics of "breakouts," which generally accompany third waves, whose personality, as discussed in Chapter 2, fills the bill.

Technical chart reading is a valid and useful approach with individual stocks. However, after years of working with the Wave Principle we find that applying classical technical analysis to the stock market as a whole sometimes gives us the feeling that we are restricting ourselves to the use of stone tools in an age of modern technology.

The class of technical analytic tools known as "indicators" are often extremely useful in judging and confirming the momentum status of the market or the psychological background which usually accompanies wave

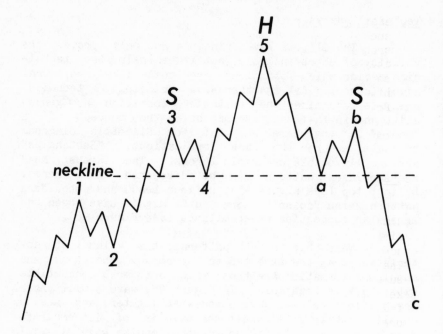

Figure 95

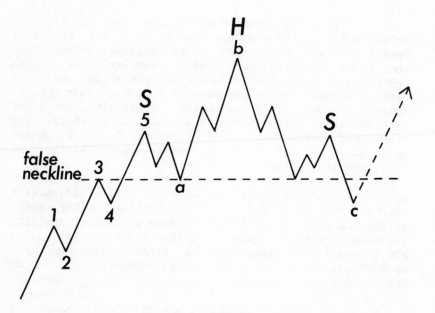

Figure 96

progression in a certain manner. Since the utility of many such indicators can change or evaporate over time, we strongly suggest their use as tools to aid in correctly counting Elliott waves but would not rely on them so strongly as to ignore wave counts of obvious portent. Indeed, the associated guidelines within the Wave Principle at times have suggested a market environment which made the temporary alteration or impotence of some market indicators predictable.

The "Economic Analysis" Approach

Currently extremely popular with institutional fund managers and advisors is the method of trying to predict the stock market by forecasting changes in the economy using interest rate trends, typical post-war business cycle behavior, rates of inflation and other measures. In our opinion, attempts to forecast the market without listening to the market itself are doomed to fail. If anything, the past shows that the market is a more reliable predictor for the economy than vice versa. Moreover, taking a long-term historical perspective, we feel strongly that while various economic conditions may be related to the stock market in certain ways during one period of time, those relationships could be subject to change seemingly without notice. For example, sometimes market declines precede recessions and sometimes they do not. Another changing relationship that comes to mind is the occurrence of inflation or deflation, which have proved bullish for the stock market in some cases and bearish for the stock market in other cases. Similarly, rising interest rates and tight money fears have kept many fund managers out of the 1978 market to date, just as the lack of such fears kept them invested during the 1962 collapse.

While Elliott claimed that the Wave Principle was manifest in all areas of human endeavor, even in the frequency of patent applications for instance, the late Hamilton Bolton specifically asserted that the Wave Principle confirmed monetary trends as far back as 1919. Walter E. White, in his work "Elliott Waves in the Stock Market," also finds wave analysis useful in interpreting the trends of monetary figures, stating that:

> The rate of inflation has been a very important influence on stock market prices during recent years. If percentage changes (from one year

earlier) in the consumer price index are
plotted, the rate of inflation from 1965 to
late 1974 appears as an Elliott 1-2-3-4-5
wave. A different cycle of inflation than in
previous post-war business cycles has developed
since 1970 and the future cyclical development
is unknown. The waves are useful, however, in
suggesting turning points, as in late 1974.

A more traditional indicator is provided by a
moving average of the weekly net free reserves
of the Federal Reserve System. Although not
always reliable as an indicator of stock market
price trends, turning points in the net free
reserve trends tend to precede turning points
in the stock market trends by about three
months. Bull markets usually occur when net
free reserves are positive or when they are
rising sharply from depressed levels. Bear
markets usually occur when net free reserves
are negative.

The Elliott wave concepts are useful in the
determination of turning points. Net free
reserves were essentially negative for about
eight years from 1966 to 1974. The termination
of the 1-2-3-4-5 Elliott down wave in late 1974
suggested a major buying point.

As testimony to the utility of wave analysis in
the money markets, we present a wave count of the price
of a long-term treasury bond, the 8 and 3/8 of the year
2000. Our price history is limited, but even in this
nine-month price pattern we see a reflection of the
Elliott process. On this chart we have three examples
of the rule of alternation, as each second wave is a
zigzag and each fourth wave a flat. The upper trendline
contains all rallies. The fifth wave constitutes an
extension, which itself is contained within a trend
channel (see Figure 97). At the current stage of interpretation, the best bond market rally in almost a year
is due quite soon.

Thus while extraordinary expenditures, credit
expansion, deficits and tight money can and do affect
prices, an Elliott pattern can always be traced in the
constantly changing levels of price movements. It is
our opinion that what influences investors in managing
their portfolios is most likely influencing bankers,
businessmen and politicians in managing affairs of the

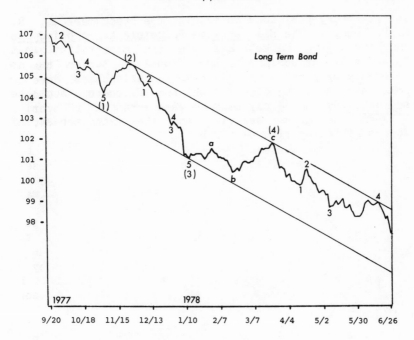

Long Term Bond

Figure 97

economy. It is difficult to separate cause from effect when the interactions of forces at all levels of activity are so numerous and intertwined. Elliott waves, as a reflection of the mass psyche, extend their influence over all categories of human behavior.

        To further complicate economic predictions upon which many market forecasts are based, exogenous forces may well be triggering cycles which man has yet to comprehend. For instance, for years analysts have traced a connection between sunspot frequency and stock market prices on the basis that magnetic radiation has an effect on investors. In 1965 Charles J. Collins published a paper entitled "An Inquiry into the Effect of Sunspot Activity on the Stock Market." Collins noted that since 1871 severe bear markets generally followed years when sunspot activity had risen above a certain level. To us, it is more than coincidence that unusually high sunspot activity has been predicted for the year 1982 by John R. Gribbon and S. H. Plagemann in their book <u>The Jupiter Effect</u>. More recently, Dr. R. Burr, in <u>Blueprint for Survival</u>, reported that he had discovered a connection between geo-physical cycles and plant life. Some analysts recently have even begun to use planetary positions to predict the stock market.   R. C. Beckman, in <u>The Elliott Wave Principle as Applied to the London Stock Market</u>, has made the observation that "sunspot cycles conform to the Fibonacci series as do movements of planets and planetary relationships in our solar system." The tie-in with the Fibonacci sequence suggests that there may be more than a random connection between stock market behavior and the extraterrestrial forces affecting life on Earth.

EIGHT

ELLIOTT SPEAKS

The Next Ten Years

While it may be quite dangerous to attempt the "impossible," a long term prediction for the stock market, we have decided to run the risk, if only to demonstrate the methods we use to analyze the position of the market in terms of the Wave Principle. The risk lies in the problem that if our thinking changes course during the next few years along with the stock market, this book will remain unaltered in its presentation of our analysis, which is based on our knowledge as of early July, 1978. We can only hope that our readers will not reject outright the theory of the Wave Principle because one rather daring prediction happens not to work out. With our reservations stated at the outset, we proceed directly to our analysis.

In Elliott terms, the Supercycle bull move begun in 1932 has nearly run its course. Currently, the market is within a bull phase of Cycle dimension, which in turn will be composed of five waves of Primary degree, two of which have likely been completed. Several conclusions can already be drawn from the long-term picture. First, stock prices should not develop a bear market downswing similar to 1969-70 or 1973-74 for several years to come, most likely not until the early or middle eighties, at least. Next, "secondary" stocks should be the leaders during the entire Cycle wave since the wave is a fifth. Finally, and perhaps most important, this Cycle wave should not develop into a steady, prolonged 1942-66 type of bull market since within a wave structure of any degree, generally only one wave develops an extension. Therefore, since 1942 to 1966 was the extended wave, the current Cycle bull market should resemble a more simple structure and a shorter time period such as the 1932-37 or 1921-29 markets.

With the DJIA in a persistent downtrend until just recently, pervasive pessimism has worked to produce several distorted "Elliott" interpretations which call for a calamitous decline to emerge from what is only a Primary second wave correction. Targets below 200 DJIA have been forecast for the near future by taking Elliott's principles and twisting them into pretzels. To such analyses, we can only quote Charles Collins from page 12 of the 1958 Elliott Wave Supplement to the Bank Credit Analyst, in which he states:

> Whenever the market gets into a bear phase, we find correspondents who think that "Elliott" can be interpreted to justify much lower prices. While "Elliott" can be interpreted with considerable latitude it still cannot be twisted entirely out of context. In other words, as in amateur vs. professional hockey, you can change some of the rules, but basically you must stick to the ground rules, or else you are in danger of creating a new game.

The most bearish allowable interpretation, as we see it, is that Cycle wave IV is not yet over, and that the final wave down is still in progress. Even given this case, the maximum expected low is 520 DJIA, the low of wave ④ in 1962. Based on the trend channel we have constructed in Figure 85 in Chapter 5 however, we have assigned this scenario a very low probability.

Basically, two plausible interpretations present themselves at the current time. Some evidence suggests the formation of a large diagonal triangle (see Figure 98) which could be constructed entirely by stampede-type swings and persistent intervening declines. Since the October 1975 low at 784.16 was broken in January 1978, leaving behind what could be a three-wave Primary advance, the diagonal triangle seems quite a plausible Cycle bull market scenario, since in a diagonal triangle each of the impulse waves is composed of three waves rather than five. Only since this Cycle wave which began in December 1974 is a fifth in the Supercycle is it possible that a large diagonal triangle is being formed. Since a diagonal triangle is essentially a weak structure, our ultimate upside target may have to be reduced to the 1700 area if this case indeed develops. To date, the drastic underperformance of the DJIA relative to the rest of the market seems to support this thesis.

The most convincing alternative to the diagonal triangle scenario is that all the action from July 1975 to March 1978 is a large A-B-C irregular correction similar to, although shorter than, the 1959-62 market pattern. This interpretation is illustrated in Figure 99 and suggests a very strong upward thrust to follow. Our 2860 target should be easily met if this interpretation turns out to be correct.

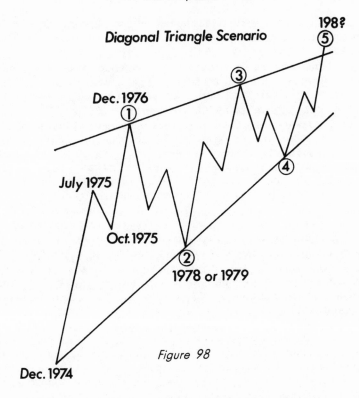

Figure 98

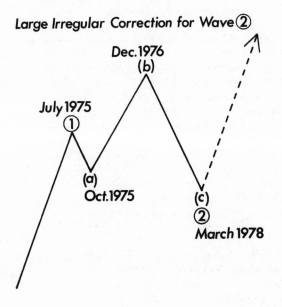

Figure 99

Our price projection for the Dow comes from the tenet that two of the impulse waves in a five-wave sequence, especially when the third is the extended wave, tend toward equality in length. For the current Cycle wave, semi-logarithmic (percentage) equivalency with wave I from 1932 to 1937 puts the orthodox high of the market close to 2860, which is quite a reasonable target, since trendline projections suggest highs in the 2500 to 3000 area. For those who think these numbers are ridiculously high, a check of back history will verify that such percentage moves in the market are not uncommon.

It is a fascinating comparison that like the nine years of "work" under the 100 level prior to the bull market of the 1920's, the last fifth Cycle wave, the Dow has currently concluded thirteen years of work under the 1000 level. And, as the Dow's orthodox peak in 1928 occurred at 296 according to Elliott's interpretation, the next peak is estimated at about the same relative level, although an irregular top could carry the averages into even higher ground temporarily. We expect the terminal point to be close to the upper Supercycle channel line. If there is a throw-over, the ensuing reaction could be breathtakingly fast.

If the interpretation of the current market status presented in Figure 99 is correct, a reasonable picture of the 1974-87 market progression could be constructed by attaching a reverse inverted image of the 1929-37 period onto the recent March 1978 low at 740, as we have done in Figure 100. This picture is only a suggestion of the profile, but it does provide five Primary waves with the fifth extending. The rule of alternation is satisfied, as wave ② is a flat and wave ④ is a zigzag. Remarkably, the rally that would be scheduled for 1986 would halt exactly on the dotted line at 740, a level whose importance already has been established (see Chapter 4). Since the 1932-37 Cycle bull market lasted five years, its addition to the current level after three years of bull market gives a length of eight years (1.618 times the length of wave I) for the current Cycle wave.

To bolster our conclusions with regard to the time element, let us first examine Fibonacci time sequences from some of the major turning points in the market, starting with 1928-29.

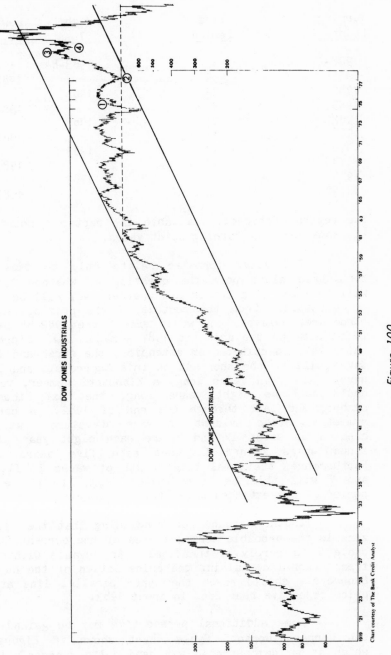

Figure 100

DOW JONES INDUSTRIALS

DOW JONES-INDUSTRIALS

Chart courtesy of The Bank Credit Analyst

Fibonacci Timetable

Turning Points	Time Period	High ?	Low ?
1928-29	55	1983-84	
1932	55		1987
1949	34	1983	
1953	34		1987
1962	21	1983	
1966	21		1987
1970	13	1983	
1974	13		1987
1974	8	1982	
1979?	8		1987

The reverse Fibonacci timetable in Chapter 4 points to the same years as turning point years.

The above formulas relate only to time and considered alone pose the question of whether 1982-84 will be a top or a bottom and whether 1987 will be a top or a bottom. From the context of the previous market structure, however, one would expect the 1982-84 period to be a major top area and 1987 a major low. Since the third wave constituted an extension, the first and fifth waves will be the shortest in this Supercycle and since wave I was five years long, a Fibonacci number, wave V could well be eight years long, the next Fibonacci number, and last through the end of 1982. A certain symmetry, often evident in wave structures, will be created if waves IV and V are each eight years long, since waves I and II were each five years long. Furthermore, the total time length of waves I, II, IV, and V will then be approximately equal to the entire period of the extended wave III.

Another ground for concluding that the 1982-84 zone is the probable terminal area of the current Supercycle V is purely arithmetical. An advance within the trend channel containing the price action of the current Supercycle should reach the upper parallel line at our price objective near 2860 in about 1983.

Some additional perspective may be gained from the Benner-Fibonacci Cycle chart shown in Figure 81 which as we demonstrated was used quite successfully in forecasting broad stock market movements from 1964 to 1974. At least for the time being, Benner's theory seems to substantiate our conclusions about the future, since at this time it clearly calls for a high in 1983 and a deep low in 1987. However, while we expect the projections to hold for the next decade, like all other cycle formulas it could very well fade in the next down Supercycle.

Even the fifty-four year economic cycle discovered by Nicolai Kondratieff, which we discussed in Chapter 7, suggests that 1987, being fifty-four years from the depression depths of 1933, would be well within a reasonable time period for some kind of stock market bottom, especially if the current plateau period generates enough optimism to allow for a strong stock market prior to that time. One of our objections to the "killer wave" occurring now or in 1979, as most cycle theorists suggest, is that the psychological state of the average investor does not seem poised for a shock of disappointment. Most important stock market collapses have come out of optimistic, high-valuation periods. Such conditions definitely do not prevail at this time, as eight years of a raging bear market have taught today's investor to be cautious, conservative and cycnical. Defensiveness is not in evidence at tops.

Finally, for those of you who have a touch of the mystic, and certainly you must if you have read this far, we would like to point out that 1983 is the Chinese year of the Pig. As we all know, bulls make money and bears make money, but pigs never do. And at the top, who will dominate the market? It makes one wonder whether George Orwell's choice of title for his book 1984 as a symbol of despair was more inspired than even he might have imagined.

O.K., what next? Are we in for another 1929 to 1932 period of chaos?

In 1929, as bids were withdrawn, "air pockets" developed in the market structure and prices tumbled precipitously. The best efforts of the leaders of the financial community could not stem the panic once the tides of emotion took control. Situations of this nature that have happened over the last two hundred years usually have been followed by three or four years of chaotic conditions in the economy and the markets. We have not seen a 1929 situation in fifty years and, while it is to be hoped that it never recurs, history suggests otherwise.

In fact, four fundamental changes in market

conditions may be part of the basis for a real panic some time in the future. First is the increasing institutional dominance of the market, greatly magnifying the impact of one man's emotions on the behavior of the market, when millions or even billions of dollars may be under the control of one man or a small committee. Second is the birth of the options market, where many "little guys" will have their stake as the market approaches its peak. In that situation, billions of dollars worth of paper assets could disappear in a day's trading on the NYSE. Third, the change in the holding period from six months to one year for declaration of long-term gains could exacerbate the "can't sell" syndrome of those who insist upon logging only long-term gains for tax purposes. Finally, the S.E.C.-mandated abolition of the specialists' role on the NYSE, which will force the securities industry to operate a dealer's market, could necessitate some brokerage firms to assume very high equity positions in order to maintain a liquid market, thus leaving them quite vulnerable in a precipitous decline.

A panic is an emotional problem, not an Elliott problem. The Wave Principle simply warns the investor of impending changes in the trend of the market for better or for worse. Deciding what to look for in the next ten years is more important than trying to predict what definitely to expect. No matter how we struggle with long-term future probabilities, our interpretations must remain tentative until the fifth Minor wave of the fifth Intermediate of the fifth Primary is underway from the 1974 low. As the "fifth of the fifth" nears its terminal point, the Elliott Wave analyst should be able to recognize the end of the Cycle bull market in stocks. In analyzing market movements under the tenets of the Wave Principle, remember that it is always the count which is the most significant. Our advice is to count correctly and never, never proceed blindly on the assumptions of a preconceived scenario. Despite the evidence presented here, <u>we will be the first to discard our predictions if the waves tell us we must</u>.

If our scenario proves correct however, a new Grand Supercycle will get underway once the current Supercycle V has terminated. The first phase could end about 1987 and bring the market down from its peak to about the 1000 level again. Eventually, the Grand Supercycle bear should carry to its expected target within the range of the previous Supercycle fourth wave, between 42 and 380 on the Dow. However, we certainly do not make any definite forecast, despite our suspicions, with respect to a panic occurring directly after the peak. The market often does move impulsively during "A" waves, but precipitous action more assuredly develops in "C" waves of A-B-C formations. Charles J. Collins, however, fears the worst when he states:

> My thought is that the end of Supercycle V will probably also witness a crisis in all the world's monetary high-jinks and Keynesian tom-foolery of the past four and one-half decades and, since No. V ends a Grand Supercycle, we then had better take to the hurricane shelters until the storm blows over.

Nature's Law

Why does man continuously have to shelter himself from hurricanes of his own making? Andrew Dickinson White's book Fiat Money Inflation in France examines in great detail a time in the past when "experience yielded to theory--plain business sense to financial metaphysics." In consternation, Henry Hazlitt, in the introduction to the book, ponders man's repeated experiments with inflation:

> Perhaps the study of other great inflations -- of John Law's experiments with credit in France between 1716 and 1720; of the history of our own Continental currency between 1775 and 1780; of the Greenbacks of our Civil War; of the great German inflation which culminated in 1923 -- would help to underscore and impress that lesson. Must we, from this appalling and repeated record, draw once more the despairing conclusion that the only thing man learns from history is that man learns nothing from history? Or have we still time enough, and sense enough, and courage enough, to be guided by these dreadful lessons of the past?

We have given this question due thought and come up with the conclusion that apparently it is one of nature's laws that man at times will refuse to accept the rest of its laws. If this assumption were untrue, the Elliott Wave Principle may never have been discovered because it may never have existed. The Wave Principle exists partly because man refuses to learn from history, because he can always be counted upon to

be led to believe that two and two can and do make
five. He can be led to believe that the laws of nature
do not exist (or more commonly, "do not apply in this
case"), that what is to be consumed need not be first
produced, that what is lent need never be paid back,
that promises are equal to substance, that paper is
gold, that benefits have no costs, that the fears which
reason supports will evaporate if they are ignored or
derided.

Panics are sudden emotional mass realizations
of reality, as are the initial upswings from the bottoms
of those panics. At these points, reason suddenly
impresses itself upon the mass psyche, saying "Things
have gone too far. The current levels are not justified
by reality." To the extent that reason is disregarded
then, will be the extent of the extremes of human emotional swings and their mirror, the market.

Of the many laws of nature, the one most
blindly ignored in the current Elliott Supercycle is
that, except in cases of family or charity, each living
thing in the natural setting either provides for its own
existence or is granted no existence. The very beauty
of nature is its functional diversity, as each living
element intertwines with the others, often providing for
many others merely by providing for itself. No living
thing other than man ever demands that its neighbors
support it because that is its right, as there is no
such right. Each tree, each flower, each bird, each
rabbit, each wolf, takes from nature that which it
provides and expects nothing from the efforts of its
living neighbors; to do so would reduce the flourishing
beauty of those neighbors, and thus of the whole of
nature in the process. One of the noblest experiments
in the history of mankind was the American structure of
human liberty and its necessary environment of free
enterprise capitalism. That concept freed men from
being bonded by others, whether they be feudal lords,
squires, kings, bishops, bureaucrats or mobs demanding
free bread and circuses. The diversity, richness and
beauty of the experiment have stood out in the annals of
history, a monument to one of the greatest laws of
nature, the final burst of achievement in the Millennium
Cycle.

The Founding Fathers of the Republic did not
choose the pyramid capped by an all-seeing eye as the
seal of the United States on a whim. They used the
Egyptian symbol of cosmic truth to proclaim the

organization of the perfect society, a society based on the knowledge of human nature and the workings of natural law. Over the past one hundred years, for political reasons, the meanings of the Founders' words have been distorted and their intentions perverted, eventually producing a social framework quite different from that established. It is ironic that the decline in the value of the dollar bill, which bears the seal of the United States, mirrors the decline in values within its social and political framework. As of this writing in fact, the dollar's value relative to that in 1913 when the Federal Reserve Board was created is twelve cents. Depreciating currencies have virtually always been accompanied by declining standards of civilization.

Our friend Richard Russell describes the problem this way:

> I firmly believe the world's troubles would be solved (and the earth would resemble heaven) if everyone would take total RESPONSIBILITY for himself. In talking to hundreds of people, I don't find that 1 in 50 holds himself up, takes responsibility for his own life, does his own thing, accepts his own pain (instead of inflicting it on others). This same refusal to take responsibility spills over into the financial sphere. Today, people insist on their right to everything--as long as you and I pay for it. There's the right to work, the right to go to college, the right to happiness, the right to three meals a day. Who promised everyone all those rights? I believe in freedom of all kinds, except where freedom becomes license and inflicts damage. But Americans confuse freedom with rights.

Lord Thomas Babington Macaulay, British historian and statesman, whom we quote in part, correctly ascertained the root of the problem over a hundred years ago in a letter to H. S. Randall of New York dated May 23rd, 1857:

> I heartily wish you a good deliverance. But my reason and my wishes are at war, and I cannot help foreboding the worst. It is quite plain that your government will never be able to restrain a distressed and discontented majority. For with you the majority is the government, and has the rich, who are always a

minority, absolutely at its mercy. The day will come when, in the State of New York, a multitude of people, none of whom had more than half a breakfast, or expects to have more than half a dinner, will choose the legislature. Is it possible to doubt what sort of legislature will be chosen? On one side is a statesman preaching patience, respect for vested rights, strict observance of public faith. On the other is a demagogue ranting about the tyranny of capitalists and usurers, and asking why anybody should be permitted to drink champagne, and to ride in a carriage while thousands of honest folk are in want of necessaries?

I seriously apprehend that you will, in some such season of adversity as I have described, do things which will prevent prosperity from returning; that you will act like people who should in a year of scarcity devour all the seedcorn, and thus make the next a year, not of scarcity, but of absolute famine. Either some Caesar or Napoleon will seize the reins of government with a strong hand, or your Republic will be as fearfully plundered and laid waste by barbarians in the twentieth century as the Roman Empire was in the fifth; with this difference, that the Huns and Vandals who ravaged the Roman Empire came from without, and that your Huns and Vandals will have been engendered within your country by your own institutions.

The function of capital (seedcorn) is to produce more capital as well as income, assuring the well-being of future generations. Once squandered through socialist spending policies, capital is gone; man can make jam out of berries but he can never reconstitute the berries.

As this century progresses, it becomes clearer that in order to satisfy the demands of some individuals and groups for the output of others, man, through the agency of the State, has begun to leech off that which he has created. He has not only mortgaged his present output, but he has mortgaged the output of future generations by eating the capital that took generations to accumulate.

In the name of a right that does not exist

within the laws of nature, man has forced acceptance of paper which represents nothing but costs everything, he has bought, spent and promised at an exponential rate, creating in the process the greatest debt pyramid in the history of the world, refusing to acknowledge that these debts must ultimately be paid in one form or another. Minimum wages that deny employment to the unskilled, socialization of schools which smothers diversity and discourages innovation, rent control that consumes housing, extortion through transfer payments and stifling regulation of markets are all man's political attempts to repeal the natural laws of economics and sociology, and thus of nature. The familiar results are crumbling buildings and rotting railroads, bored and uneducated students, reduced capital investment, reduced production, inflation, stagnation, unemployment and ultimately widespread resentment and unrest. Institutionalized policies such as these create increasing instability and have the power to turn a nation of conscientious producers into a private sector full of impatient gamblers and a public sector full of unprincipled plunderers.

When the fifth wave of the fifth wave tops out, we need not ask why it has done so. Reality, again, will be forced upon us. When the producers who are leeched upon disappear or are consumed, the leeches who remain will have lost their life support system, and the laws of nature will have to be patiently re-learned.

The trend of man's progress, as the Wave Principle points out, is ever upward. However, the path of that progress is not a straight line and never will be unless human nature, which is one of the laws of nature, is repealed. Ask any archaeologist. He knows.

APPENDIX

Mathematical Basis of Wave Theory
by Walter E. White

(Reprinted from the 1970 supplement
to the Bank Credit Analyst)

Elliott first introduced the idea that the
stock market tends to expand in a series of waves. In
previous issues of the Elliott Wave Principle, the editors pointed out that further work was necessary in
order to understand the nature of the waves and their
relation to the economy and the stock market.

In analyzing the Elliott waves, the writer has
discovered a general relationship between static form in
plant and animal life and dynamic waves of time. The
origins of this relationship may be found in fundamental
ideas of arithmetic, logic, algebra, geometry and
trigonometry dating back to 500 B.C. and of differential
and integral calculus. This general relationship
between form and waves of time is used to describe the
structure of time and the generation of dynamic waves of
time in biology, physics, geophysics, electronics, economics and other sciences. It is also used to explain
how the wave theory of time may be useful in studying
economic time series on an hourly, daily, weekly, or
annual basis.

Methods of nonlinear mathematics are used to
link the concept of shock, instability, static form and
dynamic waves of time and to help describe the structure
of time waves in the economy and the stock market, as
well as in a number of physical and biological sciences.

The idea of the shock seems fundamental and had
an influence on Niels Bohr's discovery of the process of
cognition. Bohr was a student of the philosopher Kier-
kegaard and his philosophic studies preceded his scien-
tific discoveries. Keirkegaard taught that "in life
only sudden decisions, leaps, or jerks can lead to
progress. Something decisive occurs always only by a
jerk, by a sudden turn which neither can be predicted
from its antecedents nor is determined by them." These
thoughts guided Bohr in developing atomic theory.

The concept of growth initiated by a shock may
be related to the logarithmic spiral of Figure 1 by the
simple relationship that the ratio of the length of the
arc of Figure 2 to the diameter, at any point in the

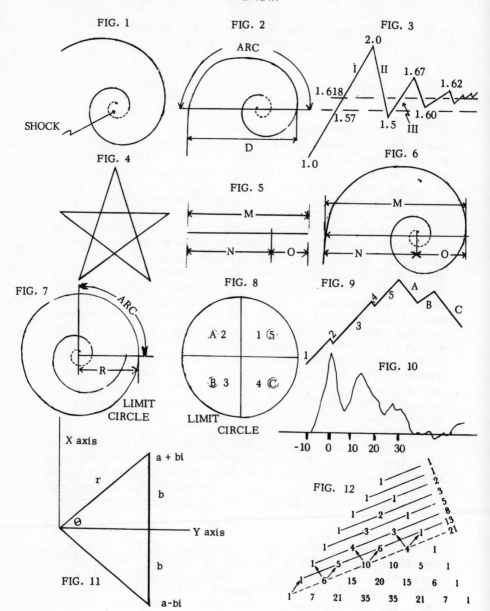

FIG. 1

SHOCK

FIG. 2

ARC

D

FIG. 3

2.0
I | II
1.618
1.57
1.67
1.62
1.5
1.60
III
1.0

FIG. 4

FIG. 5

M
N | O

FIG. 6

M
N | O

FIG. 7

ARC
R
LIMIT CIRCLE

FIG. 8

A 2 | 1 5
B 3 | 4 C
LIMIT CIRCLE

FIG. 9

1 2 3 4 5 A B C

FIG. 10

-10 0 10 20 30

X axis

a + bi
r
b
θ
Y axis
b
a-bi

FIG. 11

FIG. 12

1
1 1
1 2 1
1 3 3 1
1 4 6 4 1
1 5 10 10 5 1
1 6 15 20 15 6 1
1 7 21 35 35 21 7 1

1
2
3
5
8
13
21

evolution of the spiral, is approximately equal to the ratio of consecutive terms in the Fibonacci series (Fig. 1, 2, 3):

$$2 - 3 - 5 - 8 - 13 - 21 - 34 - 55 - 89$$

The ratio of successive terms in the above series oscillates about the limit of 1.618 as indicated in Figure 3. The value of 1.618 is sometimes designated by the Greek letter ϕ although there is no uniformity in the literature.

The number of branches in a tree increases each year in the same ratio as the ratio of successive terms in the Fibonacci series. Logarithmic spirals occur in galaxies, flowers, shells, elephants' tusks, pinecones, leaves of trees, bumps in pineapples and in many sciences. The relationships between the logarithmic spiral, the Fibonacci series and the golden ratio known for about 2500 years has been regarded as something of a mystery by many writers. One reason for the mystery is the fact that the concepts concerning the golden ratio were evolved 2000 years before the birth of Fibonacci and many centuries before the development of decimal systems. These concepts were, however, very important to the development of many ideas in arithmetic, logic, algebra, geometry and trigonometry and the same concepts may be related to the development of differential and integral calculus.

Figure 4 indicates the Badge of the Order of Pythagoras. The Pythagoreans made great progress in the theory of numbers and in the geometry of areas and solids. Pythagoras played a part in the discovery of irrational numbers when he found that no common measure can be found:

- when m is the diagonal and n is the side of a square or

- when a line m is divided in golden section into parts n and o.

Thus in Figure 5, m/n = n/o = 1.618 and this ratio is now known as the Fibonacci ratio. In the Badge shown in Figure 4, each line is cut in the golden ratio.

An algebraic proof of irrationality may be used. Since o = m - n and m/n =n/o, then m(m - n) = n squared. This equation may be solved to show that m/n = $(\sqrt{5} + 1)/2$.

Aristotle suggested an indirect proof by "reductio ad absurdum" and thus made an important step in developing the logic of mathematics.

Before decimal notations were developed, the Greeks built a ladder of whole numbers in order to approximate the irrational $\sqrt{2}$.

$$
\begin{array}{cc}
1 & 1 \\
2 & 3 \\
5 & 7 \\
12 & 17 \\
29 & 41 \\
\end{array}
$$

Each rung of the ladder contains two numbers whose ratio approaches the ratio $1/\sqrt{2}$ more closely as one moves down the ladder. The successive ratios are less than and greater than all following ratios.

A similar ladder may be constructed for any irrational. The series known later as the Fibonacci series is related to the golden ratio:

$$
\begin{array}{cc}
1 & 1 \\
1 & 2 \\
2 & 3 \\
3 & 5 \\
5 & 8 \\
\end{array}
$$

In this ladder, the right hand member of each rung is the sum of the pairs in the preceding rung. This ratio is, alternately, a little less or a little more than $(\sqrt{5} + 1)/2$ or than the golden ratio $m/n = n/o$ of Figure 5. This ladder has not been found in ancient literature but the Badge of Figure 4 suggests that the Pythagoreans were aware of this relationship. This series 1, 2, 3, 5, 8, 13 was known to Leonardo of Pisa, whose surname was Fibonacci, and this series is known as the Fibonacci series in current literature.

About 350 B.C., Eudoxus, a pupil of Plato, developed the Axiom of Archimedes by combining ladder arithmetic and the golden section of Figure 5. The whole theory of proportion for both algebra and geometry was developed from the three definitions of this Axiom.

In the logarithmic spiral of Figure 6, we find the golden ratio $m/n = n/o$ and the spiral provides a link to connect the static concepts in ancient literature with modern dynamic analysis. Nonlinear

mathematics indicates that the spiral is one of a family
of trajectories related to the stability of a system.
One main characteristic of nonlinear mathematical analysis is the existence of limit cycles. An unstable
spiral tends to approach a condition of stability indicated by the limit circle of Figure 7. The peak of one
"wave" of Figure 3 indicates an instantaneous stability
which breaks down and is followed by other attempts.
The length of the "wave" in time depends upon the intensity of the shock and the relative instability indicated
by the degree of convergence towards the ratio 1.618.
This relative instability may be explained as follows:

For the limit circle of Figure 7, the ratio of
the quarter circumference arc to the radius is $\pi/2$ or
1.57. Thus the first three waves oscillate above and
below 1.57 as well as above and below 1.618. During the
third wave, however, the upper and lower limits of 1.67
and 1.50 as indicated in Figure 3 are much closer to
1.618 than the first and second waves and, therefore,
the third wave will tend to be more stable. Later waves
converge towards the ratio 1.618 but both upper and
lower limits of these later waves will be higher than
1.57 as indicated in Figure 3.

The formation of a specific number of petals in
a flower represents one form of stability in an evolving
spiral. The number of petals corresponds to one of the
numbers in the Fibonacci series simply because the ratio
between consecutive terms in the series is the same
(approximately) as the rate of growth in time indicated
by the ratio of the arc to the radius of Figure 7.
Since we cannot have a fractional number of petals or a
fractional number of tree trunks, the Fibonacci series
represents nature's way of compromising with reality.

The ratio between the arc and the diameter of
Figure 2 is equal (approximately) to 1.618 at any point
in the evolution of the spiral and, therefore, the Fibonacci series provides a convenient method of studying
the structure of time in many phenomena. The equations
for growing and decaying spirals are:

Growth, $r = e^{bx}$ and Decay, $r = e^{-bx}$, where b is the
logarithm of the ratio of successive angles. For
rectangular coordinates in the xy plane, the corresponding equations are:

Growth, $y = e^{ax}$ and Decay, $y = e^{-ax}$, where a is the
logarithm of the ratio of successive heights of

ordinates.

When rectangular coordinates are used, each wave in time may be thought of as a tangent to a point moving along a spiral. Each $\pi/2$ or 90 degree rotation of the radius of the limit circle of Figure 7 generates a wave as indicated in Figure 9 and hesitates at a point of instantaneous stability. The waves 1, 2, 3 and 4 are shown in corresponding quadrants in Figure 8. Wave 5 is in the same quadrant as wave 1 and an extended 5 (5, 6, 7, 8) may result if the shock is strong enough. If the shock is not strong enough, an A-B-C type correction follows as indicated in Figure 9. The directions of the A, B, and C waves are the same as the directions of the 2, 3 and 4 waves respectively. The progress after wave 5 depends upon the strength of the shock and the conditions contributing to the strength of the shock must be assessed. Wave analysis alone will not provide a reliable answer.

The Fibonacci series provides a convenient measure function for the time waves of Figure 9. This measure function is expressed in whole numbers and can be used directly without reference to the basic equations listed above.

The following illustrates an interesting application in studying the pulse shapes of pulsars which have created considerable interest recently. Figure 10 is from page 418 of the April 26, 1968 issue of Science (American Association for the Advancement of Science). The author states that "Although several concepts of the object leading to two subpulses can be imagined, no schemes producing three subpulses readily present themselves."

The time structure indicates turning points at the Fibonacci numbers of 8, 13, 21 and 34 microseconds. These Fibonacci numbers, in turn, suggest that one unstable source may produce the pulse shape indicated. There are many similar applications in biology, physics, geophysics, and other sciences.

An article on page 4 of the Science Journal (Iliffe Industrial Publications, United Kingdom) states that the annual rhythm of seed germination is passed to the embryo plant in the seed by the mother plants and that this "clock" continues to keep time for as long as the seed remains viable. This is probably another example of the relations between logarithmic growth and the structure of time.

The Fibonacci series is useful in studying economic time series and these may be analyzed on an hourly, daily, weekly, monthly or annual basis. In economic time series, the origin of the shocks is complex. The resultant shock may be of national or international origin and may be due, in part, to extra-terrestrial phenomena which affect man. Correlations between solar phenomena and economic time series have been noted for more than 100 years. Recent work indicates the possibility that extraterrestrial phenomena may contribute to the shock effect on people by: a) The effects of variations in atmospheric ions on human behavior. The effect of these ions on the electro-encephalographic rhythms of the brain has been investigated and, in most people, the alpha rhythm slows (see <u>Advances in Electronics and Electron Physics</u>, Vol. 19, pp. 177-254), or b) The effects on human behavior of variations in cosmic ray intensity changes during the 11-year solar cycle. Recent experiments in space science have explained how variations in sun spots may be "transmitted" to earth via the solar wind, resulting in variations in cosmic ray intensity (see "Magnetic Fields on the Quiet Sun," November 1966 issue of the <u>Scientific American</u>; "Plasmas in Space," November 1966 issue of <u>Spectrum</u> published by the Institution of Electrical and Electronic Engineers; and "Cosmic-Ray Studies in Interplanetary Space and on the Moon," <u>Spaceflight</u>, October 1966), or c) The effects on human behavior of variations in the energy received from pulsars. The paper in <u>Science</u> mentioned above states that the radio energy emitted per unit area by the pulsar in each subpulse is equivalent in the radio spectrum to a value exceeding one-tenth that of the solar surface at all wavelengths.

The various relationships indicated by this analysis appear to support Elliott's claim that stock market movements are related to some law of nature. A study of the structure of time indicates that stock market price changes tend to develop in definite wave movements and that these movements cannot be described adequately by a random walk analysis.

The relationships between rectangular and polar coordinates may be generalized by using the concept of the complex plane a + bi introduced by Gauss. The two systems may be related as shown in Figure 11, where:

$$a = r \cos \theta$$

$$b = r \sin \theta$$

$$a + bi = r (\cos \theta + i \sin \theta)$$

$$a + bi = re^{i\theta}$$

$$dx/dt = ax - by$$

$$dy/dt = ax + by$$

where $x = e^{at} \cos bt$ and $y = e^{at} \sin bt$

If $a > 0$, the spiral unwinds and moves away from the origin; if $a < 0$, the trjectories are spirals that wind around and move towards the origin.

From the equation $a + bi = r (\cos \theta + i \sin \theta)$ and from Figure 11, we see that an imaginary number $bi = be^{\frac{\pi}{2}i}$ is a special case of a complex number $a + bi$ when the cosine side of a right triangle is equal to zero.

$$bi = be^{\frac{\pi}{2}i}$$

$$= be \cos \frac{\pi}{2} + bi \sin \frac{\pi}{2}$$

$$= 0 + bi.$$

The calculus and the imaginary are both concerned with the angle of rotation (see page 1v of "Communication, Organization and Science," Jerome Rothstein, Falcon's Wing Press, 1958). Integration corresponds to a positive rotation and differentiation to a negative rotation with respect to the reference. Differentiation represents the rotations of a tangent to a point moving along a curve. Intergration represents a reconstruction of the line from the rotations of the tangent.

$$\int^{-1} (\cos) = -\sin \qquad i^{-1}(1) = -i$$

$$\int (-\sin) = -\cos \qquad i^{-1}(-i) = -1$$

$$\int (-\cos) = \sin \qquad i^{-1}(-1) = i$$

$$\int (\sin) = \cos \qquad i^{-1}(i) = 1$$

Mathematical Induction

In the Pascal triangle of Figure 12, each term is the sum of two upper adjacent terms as indicated by the arrows. Pascal's triangle was designed to bring out the relationship between binomial coefficients and may be used in calculations of probability. Two hundred years passed before the discovery was made that the triangle contains a Fibonacci series as indicated in Figure 12. Some authorities claim that Pascal formulated the principle of mathematical induction after contemplating the triangle. Mr. D. L. Rowat, of Atomic Energy of Canada, Limited has suggested that man's thinking processes may be related to the logarithmic spiral, the Fibonacci series and the shock concept. The importance of the logarithmic spiral has been recognized for a long time. A logarithmic spiral was carved on the headboard of Isaac Newton's bed and a reference to the spiral was made on the tombstone of James Bernoulli. Goethe mentioned a spiral tendency in nature and the subject has been investigated by botanists for more than 200 years. Fractions representing the screw-like arrangement of leaves are often members of the Fibonacci series. Morning-glory buds form a corkscrew spiral.

Kepler tried to describe the distances between planets as a system in which bodies are alternately inscribed and circumscribed in spheres. The search today is for a dynamic rather than a static mathematical harmony.

Goedal demonstrated in his Proof that the resources of the human mind cannot be formalized completely and that new principles may always be found by discovery and by pragmatic methods. Goedal's Proof demonstrated, for arithmetic, that all possible relationships between whole numbers cannot be deduced from any one set of basic assumptions. The possible relationships are unlimited. Von Neumann and other intuitionists supported this approach. Elliott's early work developed from observations should be recognized as a very important step.

When this book was completed in July 1978, we had formed the following conclusions based on our reading of the Wave Principle:

1) That wave V, a tremendous bull market advance, was required in order to complete the wave structure which began in 1932 for the Dow Industrial Average.
2) That there would be no "crash of '79" and no '69-'70 or '73-'74 type decline until wave V had been completed.
3) That the 740 low in March 1978 marked the end of Primary wave ② and would not be broken on the downside.
4) That the bull market in progress would take a simple form, unlike the extended advance from 1942 to 1966.
5) That the DJIA would rise to the upper channel line and hit a target based on a 5x multiple of the wave IV low, then calculated to be 2860.
6) That, if 1974 marked the end of wave IV, the fifth wave peak would occur in the 1982-1984 time period, with 1983 being the most likely year for the actual top.
7) That "secondary" stocks would provide a leadership role throughout the advance.
8) That after wave V was completed, the ensuing crash would be the worst in U.S. history.

What surprised us since we made those arguments was how long it took the DJIA finally to lift off. The broad averages continued to rise to new highs from 1978, but the Dow, which appeared to mirror more accurately the fears of inflation, depression and international banking collapse, didn't end its corrective pattern until 1982. (For a detailed breakdown of that wave, see THE ELLIOTT WAVE THEORIST, September 1982 issue.)

We still expect our general forecasts to be fulfilled as required, although we have some refinements in the specifics, particularly the time target. As we have explained, R.N. Elliott said very little about time, and in fact our estimate for the time top was simply an educated guess based on the conclusion that wave IV in the Dow ended in 1974. Even though prices held above the 1974 low, it finally became clear that the long wave IV corrective pattern had carried all the way to 1982, and the time estimate for wave V's peak had to be shifted ahead accordingly. At no time was there a doubt that wave V would occur; it was only a matter of when, and after what.

While 1974 was correctly recognized as being the low for prices, it is now clear that the orthodox end of wave IV occurred in August 1982. The evidence for this conclusion is overwhelming.

First, as we have argued all along, the pattern from 1932 is still incomplete and requires one final rise to finish a five wave Elliott pattern. Since a Supercycle crash was not in the cards, what has occurred since 1966 is more than adequate for a correction of Cycle degree (the same degree as the 1932-1937, 1937-1942, 1942-1966 and 1966-1982 waves).

Second, the sideways pattern from 1966 pushed to the absolute limit the long term parallel trendchannel from 1932. As you can see in the illustration at the bottom of page 189, it is an occasional trait of fourth waves that they will break briefly beneath the lower boundary of the uptrend channel just prior to the onset of wave five. The price action in 1982 simply leaves no more room for the correction to continue.

Third, the pattern between 1966 and 1982 is another wonderful real-life example of standard formations outlined by Elliott over 40 years ago. The official name for this structure is a "double three" correction, which is two basic corrective patterns back-to-back. In this case the market traced out a "flat" in the first position and an "ascending triangle" in the second, with an intervening 3-wave advance, labeled "X," serving to separate the two simpler patterns. Elliott also recognized and illustrated the occasional propensity for the final wave of a triangle to fall out of the lower boundary line, as occurred in 1982.

Fourth, the pattern has some interesting properties if treated as a single formation, that is, one correction. For instance, the first wave of the formation (996 to 740) covers almost exactly the same distance as the last wave (1024 to 777). The expanding portion, moreover, takes the same time as the contracting portion, 8 years. Numerous Fibonacci relationships occur within the pattern, many of which were detailed in a Special Report of THE ELLIOTT WAVE THEORIST dated July 1982. Far more important, however, is the Fibonacci relationship of its starting and ending points to part of the preceding bull market. In Chapter 4, we discussed Hamilton Bolton's famous 1960 forecast of a Dow top at 999. But what was largely forgotten, in the wake of A.J. Frost's successful forecast for the wave IV low at 572, was Bolton's very next sentence: "Alternately, 361 points over 416 would call for 777 in the DJIA." Needless to say, 777 was nowhere to be found. That is, until August 1982. The

exact orthodox low on the hourly readings was <u>776.92</u> on
August 12. In other words, Bolton's calculations
defined precisely the beginning and end of wave IV in
advance, <u>based on their relationships to the previous
price structure</u>. In price points, 1966-1982 is .618 of
1957-1982 <u>and</u> of 1949-1956, each of which is .618 of
1957-1966, all within 1% error. All these observations
help establish that Cycle wave IV in the DJIA, which
the "Constant Dollar Dow" (see chart) clearly supports
as a single bear phase, ended in August 1982.

<u>The extent of wave V can be estimated in advance by
several Elliott methods</u>.
First, a normal fifth wave will carry, based on
Elliott's channeling methods, to the <u>upper channel
line</u>, which in this case cuts through the price action
in the 3500-4000 range in the latter half of the
1980's. Elliott noted that when a fourth wave breaks
the trendchannel, the fifth will often have a
throw-over, or a brief penetration through the same
trendchannel on the other side.
Second, the Wave Principle recognizes that there is
a tendency (not a necessity, however) that when the
third wave is extended, as was the wave from 1942 to
1966, the first and fifth waves tend toward equality in
time and magnitude. Wave I from 1932 to 1937 moved
from an estimated hourly low of 41 to an hourly peak of
194.50. Since the orthodox beginning of wave V was 777
in 1982, an equivalent multiple of 4.744 projects a
target of <u>3686</u>. The exact hourly low for 1932 is
unknown, so the "3686" number should be taken as
probably falling within 100 points of the ideal
projection (whether it comes true is another question).
Third, as far as <u>time</u> goes, the 1932-1937 market
lasted five years. Therefore, one point to be watching
for a possible market peak is 5 years from 1982, or
<u>1987</u>. Coincidentally, as we pointed out in the text,
1987 happens to be a Fibonacci <u>13</u> years from the
correction's low point in 1974, <u>21</u> years from the peak
of wave III in 1966, and <u>55</u> years from the start of
wave I in 1932. To complete the picture, 1987 is a
perfect date for the Dow to hit its 3686 target since
to reach it, the Dow would have to burst briefly
through its upper channel line in a "throw-over," which
is typical of exhaustion moves (such as the 1929
peak). Based upon a 1.618 time multiple to wave I and
upon equality to the 1920's fifth Cycle wave, an 8-year
wave V would point to 1990 as the next most likely year
for a peak. Keep in mind that in wave forecasting,
time is a consideration which is secondary to both wave

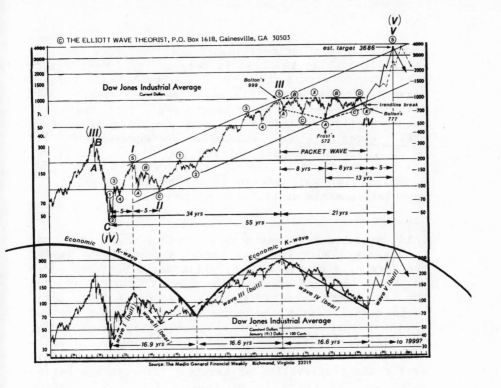

© THE ELLIOTT WAVE THEORIST, P.O. Box 1618, Gainesville, GA 30503

Dow Jones Industrial Average
Current Dollars

est. target 3686

Bolton's 999

PACKET WAVE

trendline break
Bolton's 777
Frost's 572

Source: The Media General Financial Weekly Richmond, Virginia 23219

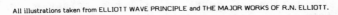

All illustrations taken from ELLIOTT WAVE PRINCIPLE and THE MAJOR WORKS OF R.N. ELLIOTT.

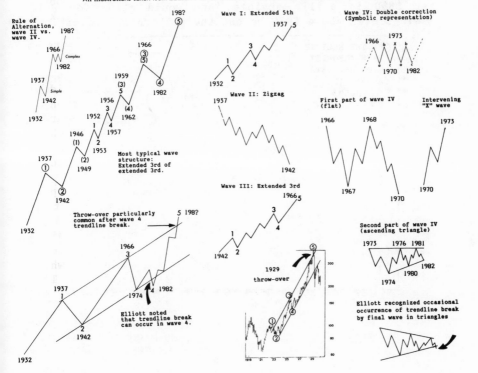

Rule of Alternation, wave II vs. wave IV.

Most typical wave structure: Extended 3rd of extended 3rd.

Throw-over particularly common after wave 4 trendline break.

Elliott noted that trendline break can occur in wave 4.

Wave I: Extended 5th

Wave II: Zigzag

Wave III: Extended 3rd

1929 throw-over

Wave IV: Double correction (Symbolic representation)

First part of wave IV (flat)

Intervening "X" wave

Second part of wave IV (ascending triangle)

Elliott recognized occasional occurrence of trendline break by final wave in triangles form, which is of primary importance, and price level.

Fourth, while the DJIA is only in its <u>first</u> Primary wave advance within Cycle wave V, the broader indexes began their own wave V in 1974, and are already well into an extended <u>third</u> Primary wave. Note that each interpretation demands three more advancing waves from 1982: waves ①, ③, and ⑤ for the Dow and waves (3) of ③, (5) of ③ and ⑤ for the others. We expect the patterns to fit together right into the final top, by which time Wall Street should be in the grip of a speculative mania of historic proportions.

Gold

Gold completed five waves up in the <u>13</u> years from 1967 to January 1980. Its bear market appears to be taking the form of a double zigzag, which would be expected to bottom in the zone of the prior wave IV ($103.50–179.50). The bear market should last <u>8</u> years, until 1987, which would coincide with the stock market peak and the end of the "plateau" phase of the Kondratieff Wave cycle. The financial difficulties then developing would again make gold the premier vehicle for investment, as well as for the preservation of assets. Although the ratios shown in the chart below support the double zigzag interpretation, a count of a large triangle beginning at $850 is still possible, and would allow for wild swings even above $850 before the pattern's termination.

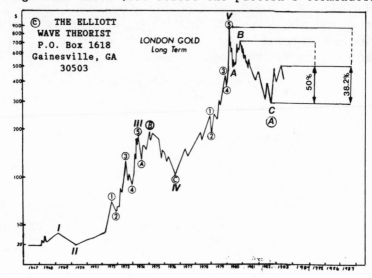

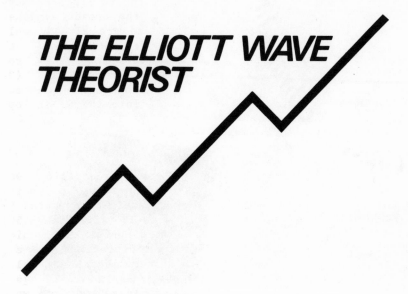

THE ELLIOTT WAVE THEORIST

THE ELLIOTT WAVE THEORIST is published exclusively for those who desire a knowledge of what the Wave Principle suggests about the current trends in financial markets. For information about this publication, contact

New Classics Library, Inc.
P.O. Box 1618
Gainesville, GA 30503

New Classics Library, Inc.

P.O. Box 1618
Gainesville, GA 30503

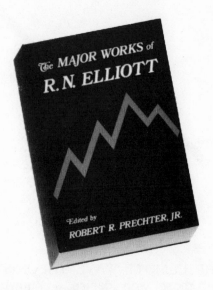

The original writings of Ralph Nelson Elliott have been assembled in one complete volume, THE MAJOR WORKS OF R. N. ELLIOTT, edited and foreworded by R. R. Prechter, Jr. The book contains "The Wave Principle" (1938), the Financial World articles (1939), "Nature's Law -- The Secret of the Universe" (1946) and the most complete biography of Mr. Elliott ever written. These historically valuable works have been out of print for decades, and previously could be obtained only in photocopied form at exhorbitant prices. This handsome 243-page hard cover volume, professionally re-illustrated, is now available from New Classics Library for $34 plus $1 postage ($7 overseas airmail).